MARTIAL ARTS

A Complete Illustrated History

MARTIAL ARTS

ARTS A Complete Illustrated History

Michael Finn

THE OVERLOOK PRESS
Woodstock, New York

Page 1: *A **tsuba,** a sword-guard for a Japanese sword.*

Page 2: *The spirit of a samurai warrior, portrayed by Toshiro Mifune.*

Page 4: *An exponent of shorinji kempo, a martial art popular throughout the Far East.*

Concept, design and editorial by
Mackenzie Publishing Limited,
178 Royal College Street, London NW1 0PS
Great Britain

Editorial: **Jeff Groman**
Design, Art Direction and Production: **Terry Allen**
Design Assistant: **Christine Nys**
Project Co-ordinator: **Christina Grant**

Published in the United States in 1988 by

The Overlook Press
Lewis Hollow Road
Woodstock, New York 12498

Library of Congress Cataloging-in-Publication Data

Finn, Michael.
    Martial arts.

    Includes index.
    1. Martial arts — History. I. Title.
GV1101.F49 1989   796.8'15   88-42773
ISBN 0-87951-335-7

CIP 88-042773

Manufactured in Italy

CONTENTS

PREFACE

The study of the Eastern martial arts has had a profound influence on my life and it may give the reader some insight to know a little about how my martial arts career began and what led me to write this book. In 1957 I was eleven years old and my passive easy-going attitude had made me vulnerable to bullying. Therefore my parents enrolled me into one of the few judo clubs of the day. I persevered and at the age of 15 took up kendo, then aikido a year or so later. Many of my early training years were spent being thrown, but as my strength grew I realized that training went far beyond winning and losing. With the little information then available I began studying the history and philosophy that lay behind training. During this learning period I was constantly rebuked for these efforts which most people considered a total waste of time.

In 1966 I joined the Metropolitan police force and, partly because of my martial arts skills, I was stationed at one of the most notorious police stations in London that had to deal with a considerable amount of violence in the area and where it was not unusual for me to be involved in anything up to 20 violent struggles a week. There I gained considerable practical experience and I found that my knowledge of the martial arts and their philosophy was invaluable. This knowledge gave me greater perception to forestall threatened violence; greater confidence often to deal with situations without resorting to anything physical myself; and, when required to use force, the ability to restrain the aggressor with minimal force on my part.

One typical incident will illustrate what I mean. At the entrance to a busy underground railway station an extremely aggressive drunk was wielding a broken bottle and threatening passers-by both physically and verbally. The public was justifiably terrified, so the officer I was with drew his truncheon and said 'the best thing to do is to hit him with this – if we move quickly he won't get us with the bottle'. I had another idea based on my martial arts experience. I circled the block and without the drunk seeing me, I managed to move up and stand right behind him. When the public saw this they all began to laugh, seeing a tall police officer behind a violent drunk. The more they laughed the more aggressive he became. I then tapped him on the shoulder. He turned, looked up, and received the shock of his life seeing me standing there. In fact he was so surprised that the bottle fell from his hands and he was arrested without any struggle. My martial arts training had taught me that fighting was a last resort and that strategy always came first.

In 1967 I won the national police judo championships, but the winning did not give me total satisfaction. I had fought since I was eleven and had come to believe that this could not be the end product: surely there was more? In 1968 I left the force and went to Japan to find out for myself.

I dedicated two years of my life to Japan and was fortunate to be taught by some of that country's best instructors. I studied judo at the Kodokan under Kotani sensei 10th dan and aikido at Waseda University under Tomiki and Oba sensei. I received kendo lessons at the government house of representatives under Hayashi sensei 9th dan; shiatsu under the founder Tokujiro Namikoshi; jojutsu under the last grandmaster of Shindo Muso Ryu, Shimizu Dai sensei 10th dan; iaido under Kuroda sensei 8th dan; and ryukyu kobudo under Suzuki sensei 7th dan. At the same time I researched deeply into the history and culture of Japan's martial traditions and received a great deal of help and friendship from perhaps the world's greatest martial arts authority, the late Donn F. Draeger.

In 1970 I returned to Britain and joined the City of London police, remaining with them for four and a half years. But my martial arts studies had become time consuming and after writing a book on police arrest techniques I left the force to establish my own martial arts school. I continued to write, train and research, sometimes travelling abroad. By 1983 I scraped together enough money to return to Japan where, sadly, some of my teachers had passed on. However, I renewed contact with others, and studied under Danzaki sensei 9th dan in iaido and was able to sit for and pass examinations that had been my goal for over 15 years. Surprisingly, it was not until my second visit to Japan that I became fully aware of the vast amount of knowledge I had accumulated over the years.

On returning to the UK I became increasingly appalled by the sensationalist attitude taken by the media concerning the martial arts, personified by such headlines as 'martial arts expert kills man with death blow', 'dangerous kung-fu spikes used at football match' and 'whirling flails of death lead martial arts exponent to court'. This picture created was vastly removed from true martial arts and the dedicated people who studied them, and it reflected badly on my endeavours and on the efforts of other serious martial arts teachers. Little wonder my training and research met so many barriers: it is always lack of knowledge and incorrect information that is at the root of such misunderstanding.

So I decided to write this book on the history of martial arts in an attempt to close that gap of misunderstanding – and I hope that it will prove both interesting and informative. Through it I have endeavoured to pass on to the reader not only the history of the martial arts, but also the Eastern attitudes and philosophies that are intangible gifts given to me by my teachers.

Acknowledgements

I would like to thank the following people, all of whom have each in their own way added and contributed something special that has made this book possible. First the masters who have imparted a special understanding of martial arts to me during my training.

The late Takaji Shimizu Dai sensei, 10th dan Jodo and the last grandmaster of Shindo Muso Ryu Jojutsu; Ichitaro Kuroda sensei, 8th dan Jodo, 8th dan Iaido, 7th dan Kendo and master of Shodo; Tsunemori Kaminoda sensei, 9th dan Jodo, 7th dan Kendo, 8th dan Iaido; the late Kenji Tomiki sensei, 8th dan and founder of Tomiki Aikido; the late Hideo Oba sensei, 7th dan of Tomiki Aikido; Sumiyuki Kotani sensei, 10th dan Kodokan Judo; Seiko Suzuki sensei, 7th dan Shito Ryu Karate, 7th dan Ryukyu

Kobudo; T. Danzaki *sensei*, 9th dan Iaido, 7th dan Kendo, 7th dan Jodo, president of the All Japan Iaido Federation; the late Hayashi *sensei*, 9th dan Kendo instructor to the Upper House in Parliament; E. Yano *sensei*, 7th dan Kendo; Kaji *sensei*, 8th dan Kendo; Y. Suzuki *sensei*, 4th dan Kendo; Tamura *sensei*, 6th dan Nihon Shorinji Kempo; Masaaki Hatsumi *sensei*, headmaster of Togakure Ryu ninjutsu; Quintin Chambers; and the late Donn Draeger *sensei*, leading authority who was qualified in numerous classical and modern martial arts.

I would also like to thank my wife Karen for her help with the manuscript; Hiroko Kawanishi for her assistance with difficult translations; and also a special thanks to Arthur Tansley, one of Japan's foremost martial arts photographers, who made so many excellent photographs in this book available.

Below: *An exponent of Eishin Ryu iaido, a style of sword-drawing performed from the seated position, prepares himself for a technique.*

*From the earliest times wise men have studied
documents that portray the principles of opposites
called* **yinyang.**

1

INTRODUCTION: THE FAR EAST

I t is the foundation on which the Far Eastern martial arts have grown, which gives them their unique mystery, power, enchantment and charisma. Understanding the Far Eastern approach to the martial arts is like having a full understanding of the life history of a mighty and ancient tree. When a tree is cut in half its trunk is composed of rings radiating from the centre and growing outwards, each ring representing a year of the tree's life. To know its age you simply count the rings — but that is not the whole story. Vital to its growth through the centuries the tree needed light, rain and nourishment, essential factors that are not apparent when we look up at a fully-grown tree.

The history of the martial arts can be seen in the same way, firstly by looking at its beginnings and then following its course outwards, taking into account the many historical and cultural factors that marked its growth. The effects down the ages of religion, philosophy, wars, persecutions, and man's constant urge to explore the unknown, are not visible when we look at the martial arts today, but nevertheless these factors played an essential part in determining their eventual form.

Mysticism, religion and philosophy

The mystery and beauty of the Far East, tempered with the primordial elements of nature, gave birth to the legendary fighting skills of the warrior. In Japan, before time itself, two deities called Izanagi and Izanami stood on the Bridge of Heaven. Reaching down Izanagi dipped his lance into the sea. As he withdrew it, small drops fell back into the ocean and coagulated to form the islands of Japan. One of the daughters of Izanami, the sun-goddess Amaterasu no mikami, was the founding figure of the national religion of Japan — Shintoism. Her grandson Jimmu Tenno became the first emperor of Japan in 660 BC, and it was believed that each successive emperor was a direct descendant of the sun-goddess. Buddhism was not introduced to Japan until AD 552 by the King of Paikche from southwest Korea. The new religion was not easily accepted, but in time it stood side by side with Shintoism.

In China man's origins can be traced to the legendary P'an ku, a being who created the world from his own body, at a time when gods and demigods ruled and the world was young. One of the first rulers under his guidance was Fu-hsi, who flourished about 2850 BC and brought into being the eight trigrams (symbols made up of three lines) called *pa-kua*, which are used in divination (fortune telling). The principal elementary forms of the trigrams are opposites such as positive and negative, or light and dark. The negative element is called *yin* and is represented by a broken line, while the positive element, known as *yang*, is represented by a solid line. All things are in a state of balance between these opposites and discord is created when that balance is disturbed. The trigrams of Fu-hsi symbolize various states of existence which reflect universal phenomena.

In about 550 BC the great Chinese sage Confucius was born. During his lifetime he made a study of the book of changes called *Yi-king (I-Ching)*, which contained the trigrams of Fu-hsi. During the lifetime of Confucius another great sage called Lao Tzu (born about 604 BC) founded Taoism, the concepts of which are based on man's efforts to find harmony with the universal forces of nature through meditation, reflected in the works called *Tao teh king*, which were attributed to him. Here was a classic example of the balance of opposites, with Confucius seeing the order of things balanced within the cultural framework of society and Lao Tzu expressing man's desire to find that order in the laws of nature reflected within himself. The philosophy of Confucianism was founded on the teachings of the classics and formulated in the Han dynasty (206 BC — AD 221). Towards the latter end of this period Buddhism was introduced to China through the trade routes from India. These beginnings were the seeds from which Far Eastern culture developed and influenced the growth of martial arts.

The birth of Buddhism

The role of Buddhism is of fundamental importance because of its profound effect on the martial arts. The birthplace of Buddhism was India, from where its beliefs had been transmitted to both China and Japan. Evidence of Buddha's life is punctuated with speculation; however records indicate that he came from an area near the Himalayas and died in 544 BC. He was the son of a king and sheltered from the miseries of the common people. One day by accident he saw human suffering, death and the sight of rotting corpses. At the age of 29 he left home and, realizing that life was transient, went in search of a truth that would remain for ever. His search continued for over six years, then one day while meditating under a tree, he experienced profound enlightenment and founded his religious teachings. The direction of enlightenment lay in the four noble truths, being the understanding of suffering, the origin of suffering, the extinction of suffering and the path that leads to that extinction. The eightfold branches of the path to the end of suffering are: right understanding, right mindedness, right speech, right action, right living, right effort, right attention and right concentration.

A parallel with knights and chivalry

Shintoism, Buddhism, Confucianism, the inception of Zen and the teachings of Lao Tzu, all these form the structure of religion and philosophy that influenced the fighting men of the Far East. By way of comparison it is interesting to look at the Christian religions to see how both man and history worldwide can be affected by religious beliefs. In Roman times Christians would face death rather than renounce their faith and many suffered ordeals beyond human endurance and survived because of their total belief in a Christian God. From 1096 to 1291, in the name of God, the holy wars against the Mohammedans were fought. It was these Crusades that nurtured the ideals of chivalry and around 1118 the order of the Knights Templar came into

Above: *Fu-hsi established the first record of the trigrams which were said to have been written on tortoiseshell.*

Below: *The ancient Chinese trigrams represent the interrelationship of opposites and the respective areas of balance in terms of natural law.*

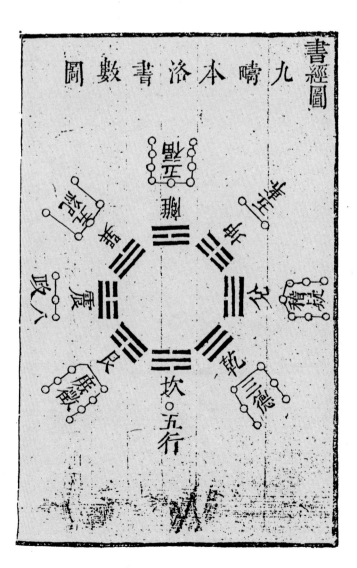

existence. These, and many similar orders of knights, such as the Hospitallers, were made up of 'religious warriors', fighting for truth, justice, God and their country. It was the age of chivalry, romance and knights in shining armour. Religion and philosophy were the uniting forces, the guiding road along which both Western and Far Eastern martial traditions grew.

A further look at the knights and their heritage will highlight other parallels and affinities with their Far Eastern counterparts. The Shaolin temples of China and the warrior monks of Japan both founded their orders on religious beliefs that were tempered with the warrior spirit. In Europe the order of Knights Templar was based on the same formula of religion and fighting skill. In Britain and Europe the knights' code of chivalry can be equated with the samurai code of *Bushido*, both reflecting the moral obligations and duties of the warrior. In Britain the warrior dream grew into the legend of King Arthur and his Knights of the Round Table, who travelled around the country righting wrongs in the name of virtue, humility, faith and purity. Fact or fiction, it is a tale that influenced the noble course of knighthood through the ages and reflects parallel principles with warrior classes such as the Japanese samurai.

It is not surprising that similarities existed between the European and Far Eastern warrior. With any warrior his success must rely on total belief in victory; any element of doubt would leave him open to his enemy's sword. To sustain this inward strength a strong philosophy was important, which was usually founded on religious teachings. To equate the role of warrior in society, as opposed to that of a thug or murderer, a personal moral discipline was needed and this grew from the same source. In physical terms the warrior had to be well trained and enduring. The incentive for the development of his skills came from the basic fact that if he was inefficient his survival time would be minimal. But strength alone never endured in combat so effective tricks and strategy grew; if these worked then they were passed on. Knowledge was gained by studying under someone who was wise in battle, which created the disciple or apprentice. The use of both weapons and empty-hand techniques served to develop an all-round fighting ability: the bow for long distance, the spear for reach, the sword for close combat, the knife and empty-hand techniques for personal combat, each skill had its area of use. However there are just so many ways you can use the hands to strike an opponent, and a limited number of directions in which you can wield a sword, so combat patterns started to emerge from both the East and the West that were sometimes similar.

Below: *The legends of the court of King Arthur portrayed the moral and spiritual values that reflect the true ideals of a warrior class.*

Above: *Since the explorations of early travellers, the Silk Route has been the link between Europe and China, the lifeline of diverse cultural exchange and the means of transporting Buddhism.*

Opposite: *The development of the Far Eastern martial arts has been overwhelmingly influenced by the history and culture of China – with Buddhism as an abiding force.*

The continental connection

Apart from similar but separate developments in martial skills through religious beliefs and the dictates of combat, many inter-cultural exchanges have occurred between East and West throughout history. For instance, the Chinese developed the stirrup in the fifth century AD, which was a major breakthrough for the cavalry as it allowed greater control and stability. The French took this idea from the Chinese in the eighth century — via Iran and Hungary — and thus this device soon spread throughout Europe.

Silk was responsible for some of the earliest exchanges between nations and many trade routes were established. The silk industry existed in India about 4000 BC and in China about 2640 BC. By AD 300 silk trading was established from China to Japan through Korea. Trade links were created between China and Europe by Alexander the Great, king of Macedon (356-323 BC). In the spring of 334 he left his homeland with an army of 40,000 men and conquered Greece, the Persian Empire and Egypt. His journey took him across Asia Minor, Persia, Northern India and as far as the Himalayas. During his lifetime, commerce, goods and cultural exchanges flowed between China and India and extended as far as Europe. The silk trade route reached out from the Black Sea through India and the Himalayas to the north China coast.

The trade routes, via both land and sea, were the links between nations and this is how knowledge was spread. However these journeys were dangerous, hard and long, often taking years to complete. Before the merchant, explorer, or seeker after knowledge set out many facts would have to be considered. Guides would be needed for the route, and protection — including self-protection — was vital. The route would be through hostile terrain and strange lands, with robbers and thieves at every turn. Academic ability and mastery of languages had to be combined with a knowledge of self-defence. There is no doubt that this is where the bond between religion and the martial skills came together.

Two famous Chinese pilgrims took the silk road to India and both returned with Buddhist scriptures. Fa Hsien made the journey in the fourth century AD and Hiuen tsaing in the seventh century, by which time about 18 schools of Buddhism existed and its teachings had extended to Central Asia. In later years legends grew around the journey of Hiuen tsaing who was said to have been escorted on his journey by four martial arts deities. Each stage of his travel was marked by violent encounters with robbers and demons, in which martial arts played an important role.

It is clear that in those times anyone undertaking a long journey, excluding the warriors, either employed bodyguards or learned to defend themselves. Merchants had the money to buy protection but the monks and pilgrims were not wealthy, so we can only surmise that they learned martial arts in order to survive, and also to protect their monasteries.

Above: *The face of a Chinese sage reflects the spiritual and cultural understanding of a nation's heritage passed down to modern times.*

The power to kill or cure

A role often played by the early transmitters of religious teachings was that of physician, the art of medicine in China, for example, being traced back to a work called *The Yellow Emperor*, written in 2697 BC. From early time martial arts have always been synonymous with the skills of healing: 'the hand that takes life also gives it'. It is important to consider this point because without the knowledge of anatomy and physiology, the skills of striking and locking and the vital areas for stabbing and thrusting could not be exploited to their full potential.

The fact that the early martial arts exponent was able both to injure and heal, makes him quite distinct from his Western counterparts. The Japanese ninja, for example, used poison darts to subdue an enemy and create the impression that he was dead, then when the time was right the enemy would be given the antidote to revive him. The ancient jujutsu masters studied *katsu*, which was a form of healing, and there is a memorable tale from the early days of judo in Japan which illustrates this dual role. In a rough area near the *kodokan* (judo headquarters), many unsuspecting members of the public were being robbed and beaten up. So a number of high-grade judo exponents decided to hide in the shadows of the dark and narrow roads in this notorious area, then send the weakest looking exponent along the street. Inevitably, when a gang of thugs set about him, all the other exponents joined in the mêlée. Limbs were dislocated and the thugs fled for their lives. The next day the thugs went to the *kodokan* to have their joints set, not knowing that the therapists were also the instigators of their injuries. The judo exponents had fun restoring their victims to health and inspecting their previous day's handywork at the same time!

The Zen factor

The balance of fighting skills, religion, healing and philosophy are the elements which consolidated into the martial arts. The first mention of martial arts as a separate entity from the act of mere fighting, is recorded as far back as the sixth century AD. There is, however, very little reliable written evidence, so legend and fact are often inseparable. A monk called Bodhidarma brought a new aspect of the Buddhist religion from India to China in about 520 AD, and this was called Zen Buddhism. The object of Zen was to find sudden enlightenment of the truth (called *satori* in Japanese), rather than through constant reading of the scriptures. There are many fanciful stories related to Bodhidarma. In one such tale he is supposed to have sat facing a wall in meditation for nine years without moving, until his legs fell off, which is why in Japan today Bodhidarma dolls have a round base and no legs. The one fact is that Bodhidarma did exist and did go to China. Significantly for our story, martial arts techniques were purported to have been taught to his monks by him, as a means of keeping them alert, fit and able to protect themselves. Thus the sixth century is noted for the beginning of Shaolin temple boxing, the name given to the fighting techniques of the Zen priests. However, it seems certain that their fighting skills existed long before this time.

Weapons from wood and steel

Man's natural weapons are his hands, feet, elbows, knees and other parts of his limbs, but the development of martial arts was not confined to just these weapons. Since early times man has sought extensions from his bodily weapons and heavy bronze mace heads have been found dating back as far as the fourth millennium BC. Even before that time primitive man doubtless used wooden clubs and stones to wage war on his enemies. All these weapons fall into two main groups: short-range and long-range. The short-range weapons include swords, spears (of the type that are not thrown), staves, daggers, halberds and so forth. The long-range weapons are the sling, bow, crossbow and the throwing spear.

In China there are records of the bow and arrow being used as far back as 500 BC but the invention had been known for at least 3,000 years previously. The archery practised in early China was also a means of spiritual and moral training — not just a method of long-range killing. The use of the Chinese sword is mentioned as far back as 206 BC and the sword, spear, crossbow, bow and arrow, and a host of other weapons were used by the Chinese infantry around 400 BC.

The Chinese bow reached Japan around the eighth century AD, but the Japanese already had their own style of bow, dating back to at least 660 BC. The early swords of Japan also came from Chinese and Korean smiths and were straight bladed. It was not until about 900 AD that the familiar curved Japanese sword came into being and that the techniques unique to the Japanese tradition began to develop. According to legend the first straight sword came from the tail of a dragon and was given to Jimmu Tenno, the first emperor of Japan, in the seventh century, as one of three sacred treasures and a sign that each successive emperor was descended from the sun-goddess.

Like the developments of empty-hand systems, many early cross-cultural links spread the use of weapons, which were accepted by other nations and adapted to their cultures. A classic example is the Okinawan weapon called *sai*, which came to the island around the fifteenth century. It found its way there from Fukien in China, where it was called the *titjio*. The weapon's origin does not rest there however. In Indonesia it was being used in the fifth century and was called a *tjbang*. Perhaps its ultimate origin lies deeper in the past — historians have yet to discover that fact.

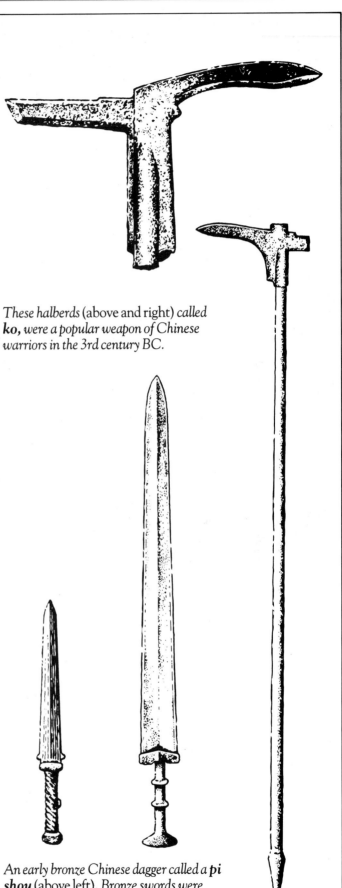

These halberds (above and right) *called* **ko,** *were a popular weapon of Chinese warriors in the 3rd century BC.*

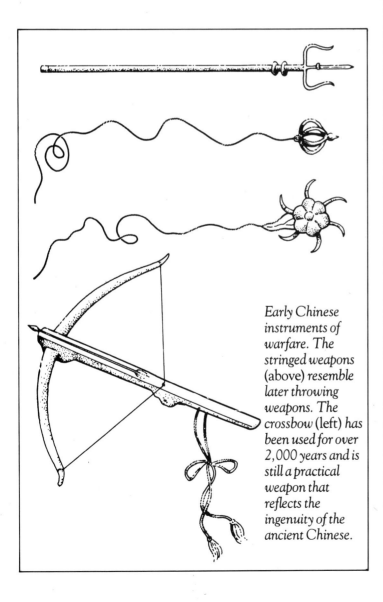

Early Chinese instruments of warfare. The stringed weapons (above) *resemble later throwing weapons. The crossbow* (left) *has been used for over 2,000 years and is still a practical weapon that reflects the ingenuity of the ancient Chinese.*

An early bronze Chinese dagger called a **pi shou** (above left). *Bronze swords were popular in China between the 5th and 2nd centuries BC* (above right).

The rise of Japan's samurai

In Japan's early history local landowners employed men to protect their property, hence the word 'samurai' came into being from 'sameru' which means 'to serve' and was used to describe these warriors. By about AD 650 Buddhism had gained national recognition alongside Shintoism, and Chinese culture began to dominate many of the nation's aspects. By the beginning of the twelfth century the warrior class had begun to grow and even the Buddhist monks were able to assemble formidable armies to protect their interests. Many powerful clans sprang up, each reaching for power under the favours of the emperor. For a while the Taira clan held the balance of power but the opposing Minamoto clan, led by Yoritomo, won a decisive victory at the battle of Dannoura on 25 April 1185.

Yoritomo became military ruler of Japan and set up his capital in Kamakura. Because of his frugal living and love of the warrior class, this period became a golden age for the Japanese martial arts. The warriors became known as *bushi* — not samurai — and codes of ethics called the codes of Bushido were formulated. Unlike China, the Japanese *bushi* had a status at the top of the social scale; they had the right to bear arms, administer justice and even take life. Schools of martial study began to develop, called *ryu*, and these taught a variety of weapons and empty-hand skills, instruction on battle strategy and other subjects.

Japan saw many centuries of bloody civil war, comparative peace not coming until the end of the sixteenth century. This was as a result of the efforts of three great generals called Nobunaga, Hideyoshi and Ieyasu, the Japanese likening their very different approaches to the song of the nightingale. It was said that if a nightingale would not sing Nobunaga would kill it, Hideyoshi would make it sing and Ieyasu would wait until it did sing. Their united effort brought Japan under one rule, but the feudal era did not end until about 1867 and the skills of the samurai flourished.

As Japan fell into line with the Western world, by accepting a modern conscript army and system of government, the now neglected samurai felt increasing pressure on their status. This discontent at the new administration culminated in a rebellion led by Saigo Takamori, a noted statesman of the time. The final stand of the samurai, in 1877, was called the Satsuma rebellion, in which some 40,000 warriors with traditional weapons waged war against a modern conscript army with modern firepower. Amazingly the fighting lasted for over seven months but the slaughter of 30,000 men and the death of Takamori, who took his life on the battlefield, saw a final end to the samurai struggle and the dawn of a new era.

From that period until modern times the combative aspects of martial arts took on a new image, accelerated after World War II, with the change in emphasis from victory in combat towards self-perfection through training.

The fighting monks of China

Chinese history has been marked by many wars. In the early thirteenth century the mongol Ghengis Khan invaded China and in 1279 Kublai Khan became emperor of China, the mixture of the two nations further affecting the development of the Chinese martial skills. During Kublai's rule the doors to foreign trade were opened and European nations flooded in, but after his reign ended a great hatred grew towards foreigners and the borders were sealed.

It was not uncommon throughout China's feudal history for the monasteries to supply fighting men for the emperor's wars, nor was it uncommon for the emperor to raze a monastery to the ground at the slightest hint of sedition. In the seventeenth century the Manchus invaded China and destroyed at least two leading Shaolin temples. Hate grew among the monks and many secret organizations began to flourish, directed at overthrowing the Manchu rule. During this time — against the background of numerous rebellions — the martial traditions flourished.

At the turn of the twentieth century, amidst political and social unrest and with the encouragement of the empress dowager, the Boxers (monks trained in the martial arts) rose up against the foreigners in China. One of the main groups involved in this resurgence was the I Ho T'uan (Righteous Harmony Fist). It was believed by the Chinese people that the Boxers were invincible, even to modern firepower. This reputation was due in part to their notorious victories against all odds and to their use of various rituals and induced self-hypnotic states. However, the popular belief of the Chinese Boxers' powers were dented when in 1899 a large group of them was executed by a firing squad in Shantung. On 17 June 1900, on the orders of the empress dowager, the Boxers led a rebellion to kill all foreigners in China. Peking was taken under siege and the aliens took refuge in a Catholic cathedral. Peking was returned to foreign control that August, but not before many thousands had been slaughtered.

After the defeat of the Boxer Rebellion, the various Boxer groups fragmented, some venturing to Taiwan and other areas. At the time of World War I, many Chinese Boxers united with local warlords throughout the Chinese nation and by 1930 associations proliferated which encouraged the healthy activities of the Boxers' skills as a means of physical culture. However, with the founding of the Communist regime in 1949, many Boxers escaped to Hong Kong, Malaya and other safe territories, and continued to practise and teach their fighting skills.

The author is acquainted with the exploits of one old man who practised a system known as 'spider style'. As a young man he left China to escape communism and went to live in the jungles of Malaya, where he still exists off the land and practises his skills. During his early days in the martial arts, he challenged a master of spider style. In those times a master would set up in a town or village and light a three-day candle. While it burned anyone in that village could challenge him, but by the time it went out he was either accepted, defeated or dead. The challenger lost his contest but became a disciple of the master and in the process of time learned 18 of the master's 36 forms. In his lifetime the old man has killed a number of challengers who have threatened his existence.

Left: *Artist Kunisada's portrayal of the empress Jingo Kogu with one of her ministers is a vivid evocation of samurai splendour.*

Following pages: *During the Boxer Rebellion at the turn of this century the fanatical Boxers showed no mercy to the foreign forces they vanquished.*

The eternal past

At the beginning of the twentieth century both Japan and China were just emerging from the feudal era. Well over a hundred years before, with Britain as the pioneer, the Western world had shed its feudal shroud and entered the industrial age, during which all remnants of martial tradition and feudal combat were eventually buried forever beneath modern military growth. The new technology spurned the cultural heritage of the past. A new age had dawned — one that the Far East had yet to enter.

It was because of this late emergence from the feudal period, together with other social and political changes, that the Far East retained its cultural traditions — including martial arts — for so long. In both Japan and China today we can see martial arts that were actually practised hundreds of years ago, together with modern fighting skills derived from the ancient sources. Modern technology and the industrial age, particularly in Japan, have grown around these old traditions and not buried them. In fact the strength that has forged the new industrial growth in Japan has its roots in the very heart of the martial arts. The unity, sense of duty, obligation to the nation above self and the striving for perfection, are the codes of both the samurai and the worker in today's Japan.

The strategy and interplay of Japan's businessmen is a reflection of the classical schools of the samurai. In fact many Western businessmen are familiar with *A Book of Five Rings*, written by the famous sixteenth-century Japanese swordsman Miyamoto Musashi. The strategies that apply to swordsmanship also apply to modern business. The skills of the feudal warriors of the Far East are still significant in modern times.

Left: Shinto is Japan's indigenous religion. The top character (**shin**) means god and the lower character (**to** or **do**) means the way. Thus Shinto means the way of the gods.

Opposite above: Symbols of Shintoism can be seen throughout Japan. Here a newborn baby is being presented at a Shinto shrine.

Opposite below: Although Japan is one of the modern world's leading industrial nations, the technology of the industrial age has grown around the old traditions and not destroyed them.

*At the heart of the classical **ryu** – beyond technique – lay subtle strategy.*

2

WARRIOR STRATEGY AND PHILOSOPHY

Before we begin to look at the philosophy and strategy of the warrior, let us first define what we really mean when we use the terms 'a martial arts exponent', or 'martial arts'.

Any martial skill which is not beneficial to both the exponent and society is not a martial art. A thug may use a martial art technique in a fight but this does not make him a martial artist: had he been taught true martial arts he would not be a thug. Martial arts training is not just the learning of skilled fighting techniques; there must be disciplined training, a moral philosophy, dedication, a sense of duty and respect. This concept is best expressed by the Japanese character for martial, which is 'bu'. It is used in such expressions as 'budo', which means martial ways, and 'bushi', a samurai warrior. The character is made of two sections, the inside part meaning 'tomaru' (to stop) and the outside section representing a warrior with a spear. Thus the aggressive warrior who wants to cause violence and disorder with the spear is prevented from doing so by the other warrior expressed by 'tomaru'. What this conveys is that the weak cannot prevent violence, the strong gain everything by force, but the warrior whose strength is tempered by moral duty, can prevent violence simply by his presence, without raising a finger.

A martial art is a classical fighting system in which the emphasis is on victory in combat, but which has the secondary motivation of self-perfection through training and includes a moral duty to society. A martial way describes a martial skill that has the main motivation of self-development through training, with a possible secondary consideration of practical use. A martial sport describes a martial activity in which exponents compete within a set of rules and in so doing develop a healthy mind, body and spirit.

Pure strategy

The highest ideal in fighting is winning the encounter without resorting to violence, that is by pure strategy. The samurai and the Chinese Boxer were both exponents of martial arts. In the turbulent days of the feudal period, their main consideration was victory in combat and this was not won by technique alone: strategy also had to be employed. One account of pure strategy was related in the tale of the sixteenth-century samurai called Tsukahara Bokuden. One day he was on a small ferry, crossing one of Japan's inland seas. One of the other passengers was a loud-mouthed samurai worse the wear for drink. Having intimidated everyone with his attitude he spied Bokuden sitting passively in a

Left: This **kanji** *(character), meaning* **budo** *(martial way), was written by the renowned calligrapher and master of martial arts Ichitaro Kuroda* **sensei.**

corner. 'Hey you', he bawled across the ferry, 'I see you have two fine swords, but can you use them?' The boat became still as all the passengers fell into apprehensive silence. After a pause Bokuden replied: 'my fighting style is of the highest level, not only do I not need my swords, but I don't use my hands either.' The braggart, thinking this to be an insult, challenged Bokuden to a match. Bokuden said he would not fight in the confines of a small ferry in case innocent people were killed, so he pointed to a small island and ordered the ferryman to pull in there. The drunken samurai was so incensed by the insult that as soon as the boat touched the shore he jumped out and drew his sword. Quick as a flash Bokuden snatched the oar from the ferryman and pushed the boat out to sea. The irate Samurai ranted and raved on the island but as he became a speck in the distance, Bokuden shouted back: 'this is the style of fighting without using the hands!'

In the history of Far Eastern martial arts thousands of books have been written on the subject of strategy, but as far as the warrior was concerned there was one main reference source for

most of these. This work, written in China by Sun Tzu in about 400 BC, is called *The Art of War* and is still recommended reading in military academies throughout the world, because it covers every aspect of strategy, from spy networks to field tactics.

There are many legends about this remarkable man. On one occasion Sun Tzu offered his services to the king of his province as a military adviser. The king, with some audacity, put him to the test by ordering him to drill the palace concubines. Sun Tzu agreed to this on the understanding that he would have complete control over them. As he tried to drill the women they all began to laugh and giggle. He put this down to the fact that his orders were not explicit enough and tried again, giving them clear directions on marching and drilling. But none of them took him seriously and again they began to giggle and laugh. Sun Tzu then selected two of the women (who happened to be favourites of the king) and ordered them to be beheaded. Despite protests from the king, the sentence was carried out. After this the reality of death caused the other women to take his orders very seriously and soon they were turned into well-disciplined troops.

The art of estimation

One important aspect of battlefield strategy is the art of estimation, for such factors as weather conditions, the number of enemy troops, and the state of the enemy's morale. *The Art Of War* advises on these and other matters, and a story which reflects the true importance of estimation relates to the great sixteenth-century Japanese commander Takeda Shingen, who was guided by the teachings of Sun Tzu. When Shingen was a child of ten, he once played the 'shell game' with children of other local lords. In this game, a bag of shells was emptied on to the floor, each player estimating the total number. Some said there were ten thousand, others five thousand or four thousand, but Shingen was quite sure there was a total of three thousand three hundred. When the shells were counted it was found that Shingen was exactly right. He was then purported to have said: 'If you estimate like this, I would not need many warriors to defeat you in war'.

In the seventh century a Japanese prince named Shotoku, who was well read in the Chinese classics, was revered for his judgements in the administration of justice in court cases. To help him, he employed what later became known as ninja (spies) to secretly look into the background of the litigants and find out the truth, so that when judgement was to be made he would know who was lying. The teachings of Sun Tzu did not escape the ninja, who established vast spy networks based on his studies.

Victory through strategy rather then brute force and ignorance was always a preferable way for the true warrior, and is a vital component of the martial arts. Confucius confirmed this principle during discourse with a pupil, when he expressed the opinion that it was better to be on the side of the person who sought victory through strategy rather than violent abandonment. Strategy blew the winds of fate in a decisive direction for Yoritomo, the twelfth-century Japanese general who established the nation's first military rule. His battle for power was against the Taira clan who stood in his way and the final confrontation came with the battle of Dan No Ura, which are the straits between the islands of Honshu and Kyushu. In this battle, both strategy and the power of estimation played important roles.

The Taira clan were renowned sailors and made use of this ability by waging a sea battle in the straits of Dan No Ura, thus fighting in a familiar environment. The Minamoto clan, led by Yoritomo, were in the process of being defeated by the Taira fleet when they employed a strategy which quite literally changed the tide of misfortune. Yoritomo obtained information about the weather conditions and tides in the area, then awaited his opportunity to attack when the tides turned in an outward direction. His brother Yoshitsune ordered his men to aim all their arrows at the helmsmen of the Taira boats. When Yoritomo began his attack, the Taira boats were driven back with the tide, the death of the ships' helmsmen causing total confusion as boats went out of control and were wrecked on the rocky shores of Dan No Ura. Minamoto's troops soon dispatched the survivors.

The above account of brilliant strategy has parallels with the Chinese account of Sun Pin's strategy many hundreds of years before. Sun Pin estimated the arrival of enemy troops on the road to Ma Ling and ordered his men to strip a tree and carve the name of the enemy commander in big characters upon it. He then ordered all his troops to direct their arrows at the tree and shoot when they saw a lighted torch. As dusk drew in the enemy troops arrived at the tree, saw the sign and told the commander, who was consumed with curiosity and approached the tree. As he held a torch up, his body was riddled with thousands of arrows. His troops fell into confusion at the loss of their leader and were defeated.

The works of Sun Tzu set a foundation on which fighting men for centuries after were to establish their strategies. The already mentioned Japanese commander Takeda Shingen was renowned for his ruthless strategy, and even as a teenager he proved worthy as a great general. On his first campaign with his father they besieged an enemy castle, but as winter drew on and weather conditions worsened, Shingen's father decided to retreat, leaving his son and a few hundred men as a rearguard. However, Shingen was impatient and decided to precipitate the castle's capture. When his father had gone, he hid all his men and waited. The scouts from the castle reported back that the coast was clear and that the enemy had fled; then the defenders began a feast to celebrate their victory. That night, when everyone in the castle was in a drunken stupor, Shingen attacked with his few hundred men. The defenders thought that the attackers had returned in force and in the state of confusion that was created over 2,000 of them were slaughtered by Shingen's small rearguard. Later, Shingen adopted the motto of Sun Tzu for his emblem: 'Swift as the wind; Still like the forest; Invading like fire; Immovable as the mountain'.

Following pages: The battles of the Minamoto clan, led by brothers Yoritomo and Yoshitsune, against the Taira clan, have offered Japanese artists a never-ending source of material. This woodcut masterpiece by Kuniyoshi portrays ghosts attacking the winner's ship from all sides.

The fighting style of Musashi

One warrior who defined his own path of strategy was the sixteenth-century samurai Miyamoto Musashi. At the end of his lifetime he was purported to have completed his work called *Gorin no Sho* (Book of Five Rings). It contains five chapters, each one describing strategy in relation to the five elements of earth, water, fire, wind and air. Musashi's father specialized in a weapon called a *jutte*, an iron truncheon often used by Japan's feudal police force. Musashi had complete contempt for his father's attraction to this weapon as opposed to the sword and at the age of nine he was considered wayward and sent to a Buddhist temple to be looked after.

Musashi's encounters in combat all reflect the directness of Zen, but not the compassion of Buddhism. His first match was at the age of thirteen, when he put his name forward to fight a swordsman called Arima Kihei, who was offering challenges in the area. When Kihei saw that his opponent was just a boy armed only with a wooden practice sword, he spat at the boy and rebuked him. In an instant, Musashi took advantage of the moment of unawareness and caved Kihei's skull in with one blow of his wooden sword. As Kihei fell dying to the ground, the young Musashi continued to beat his head to pulp.

Musashi became well known for his fighting style of using two swords and had an undefeated record in combat. When he was 21 he visited Kyoto to challenge Seijuro, the master of the Yoshioka school of martial arts. However, Musashi had a problem in that all challenges were accepted by senior teachers, never by the master. In this way there was no loss of face for the master if one of his exponents was defeated. The Yoshioka school had the patronage of the important Ashikaga family who were held in high esteem — so there was a great deal at stake. Musashi defeated Seijuro's strategy by making a public announcement that the match was to take place between him and Seijuro in person. He then put up posters to this effect throughout Kyoto. If Seijuro had backed down at this point, he would have lost face, so the match went ahead.

A challenge of skill between exponents was a formal matter, during which strict etiquette was observed. On the appointed day Seijuro attended the area set out for the contest, dressed in a formal kimono and carrying his sword at his side. A huge crowd had gathered to see the event and as dawn began to break across the sky, the time for the encounter was at hand. Dawn broke, the sky lightened and birds sang to herald a new day — but still Musashi did not appear and Seijuro waited until impatience was about to explode inside him. Still Musashi did not show his face.

In fact, at this moment Musashi was in the crowd only a short distance from Seijuro, but no one noticed him. Musashi was dressed in an informal way, more suited to a stroll in the park than for a contest, and at his side all he carried was a wooden practice sword. As Musashi stepped from the crowd, Seijuro was confused by his appearance. This total change from the correct order of things, together with his mounting impatience, was too much for Seijuro. He drew his long sword and in a rage attacked Musashi with a downward cut to the head. In true martial arts, timing defeats speed. Musashi brought his wooden sword slowly upwards in a powerful crushing blow under Seijuro's chin. The impact killed Seijuro instantly and in the confusion Musashi made his escape before any of the master's students could seek instant revenge.

In the book *Gorin no Sho* Musashi says that a violent mind wields a careless sword and it was this state of mind that Musashi had created within his opponent by turning up late. Perhaps also Seijuro had forgotten the power of a wooden sword and underestimated Musashi's ability because of his dress and appearance. Musashi was a great exploiter of human nature and had developed an inborn sixth sense about timing — as his next encounter proved.

After the death of Seijuro the members of the Yoshioka school suffered a great loss of face and various efforts to regain their honour were attempted. Musashi, on the other hand, as news of his encounter spread, had risen from an almost unknown samurai to local folk hero. In the end the chance of honour fell upon the ten-year-old son of Seijuro and a challenge was arranged between Musashi and the young lad. The meeting place for the challenge was the Ichijoji temple near Kyoto. Here the exponents of the Yoshioka school plotted to help the young boy avenge his father's death by jointly fighting Musashi.

As with the previous challenge, the match was arranged for dawn. The young boy and his helpers arrived and prepared for the encounter while the mantle of darkness framed the stillness in night shadows. Unknown to them, Musashi had already studied the terrain and was in a tall pine tree above them. When dawn heralded the start of the challenge everyone expected Musashi to arrive late in his usual manner, so they settled down to wait. The cicadas chirruped their song, the warmth of the day filled the air and small flies began to buzz around the trees. As the young boy started to prepare for the late arrival of Musashi, suddenly from above him his opponent sprang down from the tree. Even before the boy had glanced up, his head was severed from his body and spun upwards in the air. His followers were so amazed at this sudden appearance and the ferocity of the attack on the boy, that it was a few moments before they gave chase. Musashi had a good start and cut down those who reached him first. He chose the narrow paths between the rice fields and thus limited the ability of his attackers' power to reach him. After felling a good number of them, Musashi escaped.

Timing was the essence of Musashi's strategy, complemented with surprise. There is timing in all things, the seasons, the tides and the life cycle of man. There is timing in music, the balance of the individual instruments creating the harmony of rhythm: the more perfect the rhythm the easier a wrong note is spotted. The musician perfects this skill so that harmony and rhythm are intuitive, for there is only the smallest part of a second between the right and wrong note, between life and death or between the killing sword and the failing sword. Musashi perfected his sword skills; he knew his enemy would misjudge his timing and expect him to arrive late; and he knew his escape route allowed only one attacker at a time. Thus he became the conductor and his enemy the orchestra that played his tune of death.

Right: *A page from the book of strategy called* **A Book of Five Rings,** *written by the sixteenth-century swordsman Miyamoto Musashi and still read today in both East and West.*

はしがき

『五輪書』は、宮本武蔵（一五八四～一六四五年）自身が二天一流について書き残したものである。

その剣の心は、武士道と結びつけられ、永く封建道徳の支柱となってきた。だが、今日、封建道徳のおもしを取り去ってこれを読むと、わたしたちは、その生き生きした姿を再発見することができる。それは、おどろくほどの新鮮さをもっているのである。

もともと剣術は敵を倒す実技として発生した。相手を倒すには彼我の関係において精神と技術を最も有効にコントロールしなければならない。『五輪書』は、そのための実利、実用の書なのである。

武蔵は実践的求道によって、ドライなまでの合理性を身につけ、それを書いているのである。

この意味で『五輪書』は、きわめて今日性をもっている。今日はまた、ある意味で、きびしい勝負の時代だからである。もちろん、武蔵の生きて戦った時代と今日のそれとを同一視し、『五輪書』を教典扱いにすることはナンセンスにひとしい。だが、わたしたちは、食うか食われるかの時代に生きぬこうとするわたしたちは、武蔵の勝負道から合理精神をくみとり、今日に活用することがで

A great general and leader

One of Japan's greatest strategists was born towards the end of the thirteenth century. His name was Kusunoki Masashige and he was loyal to the emperor Go-daigo. Even as a child Masashige displayed exceptional powers in the skills of strategy. He carved a turtle out of wood and told his playmates that he could control it with the god-like powers he possessed. In fact he had secured a loach (a type of fish) to the underside of the wooden turtle. As he placed it in the water, the wooden turtle began to swim and move, apparently at his will. All the other children held him in awe, until he revealed to them how they had been tricked.

When Masashige came of age as a warrior he fought on the side of the emperor against the armies of the Hojo military dictatorship, his most noted campaign being in defence of Chihaya-jo, a castle in the area of Yamoto in southern Honshu, where with only a few thousand men he is recorded as having defeated hundreds of thousands. He set up two strongholds, one was the castle of Akasaka and the other was Chihaya castle. After a bloody battle that lasted for six days, the water supply of Akasaka was cut off and it fell to the enemy. This did not deter Masashige as he had already planned for the enemy's assault on Chihaya. This castle had been well chosen: it was inaccessible to large bodies of troops who had to ascend the Kongo mountain range and fight in the rocky terrain that Masashige knew so well. Also, there was no shortage of water, since the castle contained a secret spring known only to a few mountain priests, and it was well stocked with provisions. So the defenders waited for the assault, ready to unleash the surprises that Masashige had in store for the enemy.

It is said that when all the enemy forces were gathered, some 800,000 joined in the attack. Only a truly great general could defend against such odds, but Masashige had already turned their large numbers to disadvantage, because only small parties could assail the castle at any one time. As the first groups attacked, large rocks and boulders were hurled down upon them and it is recorded that over 6,000 of the enemy died in the first day of fighting. In the next assault, the attackers were allowed to come as far as the ditches that surrounded the castle and were once again lured into a trap. Above the ditches Masashige had prepared many felled trees, which were released and rolled down upon the enemy. Those who had not fled or been crushed were taken by arrows from the castle walls, and another 5,000 men were lost.

The enemy then decided to starve the warriors from the castle and laid siege. The result of this strategy was a discontented and uncomfortable enemy — facing Masashige's well-fed and snug army. However, Masashige knew that he must draw the enemy's attack on the castle once again, so under the cover of darkness he sent his men out to place straw figures, dressed as warriors, at the foot of the castle. As daybreak came, the enemy saw the shapes of warriors in the mist beneath the castle. Thinking that the besieged army had amassed for a final confrontation, they made their charge. Arrows rained down on the straw figures, but by the time the attackers were close enough to realize their mistake it was too late. Boulders and arrows from the castle decimated their forces even further.

With discontent growing, the enemy planned their last attack. A giant bridge was constructed which spanned a deep ravine between the castle and its assailants. Believing they were at last on their way to victory, thousands of troops began to pour across the bridge. Here again Masashige displayed his military genius. He ordered his men to pump oil on to the bridge and when this was done burning torches were thrown upon it. Strong mountain winds ensured a swift conflagration and once again thousands of men perished. This was the final confrontation and the enemy troops withdrew and fled.

Left: A legendary confrontation between Miyamoto Musashi and a giant bat, from the 'Sixty-nine Stations of Kisokaido' by Kuniyoshi.

Below: One of medieval Japan's greatest strategists, Kusunoki Masashige, whose loyalty to the emperor Go-daigo led to his inevitable death.

The philosophy of the warrior

There are many tales of warrior strategy both on the battlefield and in individual combat, but warrior philosophy was equally important. Whether Shinto, Buddhist, Taoist or Confucian, the sincerity and understanding of the chosen path affected respective outlooks quite dramatically. It is hard to pinpoint any totally distinct examples of pure religious influence, because ancient history is nebulous and the various religious philosophies have overlapped and affected one another. It is important, however, to recognize the fact that the separate entities of strategy, skill and philosophy represent the primary structure of the warrior mind, philosophy representing the role of counsellor, moralist, spiritual strengthener and giver of insight.

In Japan during the reign of the emperor Go-daigo (1318-39), a revived Confucianist philosophy was introduced from China. This was encouraged by the emperor because it adhered to the understanding of the strict structure of things, for example the total unquestioning loyalty of subject to ruler or servant to lord. One man who followed this teaching was Kusunoki Masashige, who upheld his beliefs even in the face of death.

Some time after the siege of Chihaya castle Masashige was summoned to attend Go-daigo. The son of Hojo Takatoki had rallied a great number of troops in the southern island of Kyushu, with the intention of forcing a final confrontation in the capital of Kyoto. Go-daigo wanted Masashige to forestall this attack by going to meet the enemy armies, but Masashige suggested a more effective strategy by luring the enemy into Kyoto and attacking them from both sides. However, despite Masashige's protestations, the emperor ordered him to meet the enemy and make a direct attack. Although Masashige knew the plan would fail, he remained loyal to the emperor and carried out his wishes.

This Confucian attitude is both tragic and beautiful at the same time. Knowing that he was doomed, Masashige instructed his son on the conduct of affairs after his death and bade farewell to his family for the last time. The outcome was inevitable. After the crushing defeat of Go-daigo's army the few survivors took refuge in a house and it was there that Masashige and his brother took their own lives to prevent capture. To Masashige his philosophy was not just a word: it was a way of life and death.

Where Confuciansism expressed duty and obligation, in Masashige's case even to the point of death, Zen expressed the instant truth that helped accept the reality of death. Zen began to influence the Japanese during the thirteenth century and was particularly popular with the warrior class because there were few scriptures to study and it dealt with the reality of the present. It released the warrior from worries and anxieties that inhibited him from responding instantly as a fighter.

The principle of Zen is as simple to understand as a leaf falling from a tree — it just happens. The ordinary warrior who confronts an enemy in the face of death will have a thousand thoughts rushing through his mind: will I win, shall I cut quickly with my sword, perhaps I must leave an opening for my enemy and seize my chance to kill him when he goes for it? While his mind is busy, the enemy will attack and the warrior will be defeated. The mind of the Zen disciple is like an empty cup waiting to be filled, responding to the present, not manacled by thoughts of the future. The attack comes, the response is made, the enemy is dead, there is no more — it just happens.

One aspect of Zen philosophy is what is known as 'the cleaving of attachment'. If something happens that catches and holds your attention, you will not win. If the warrior's mind remained solely with the technique he was performing, he would not win. In simple terms, he has to respond to change, the act and the response being instant, like a reflection in a mirror. Munenori, a famous Japanese sword master, once said: 'one mind sees everything and in this way many things are controlled by the one mind.'

The Zen philosophy was brought to China by the monk Bodhidarma in the sixth century AD and his teachings influenced the training of the Chinese Boxers from the Shaolin temples. By the thirteenth century the same Zen teachings were also affecting the philosophy of the samurai classes in Japan. When the first Zen monks came to Japan they could speak very little Japanese, so teachings were passed on at a more intuitive level. The master would set a problem or riddle, using very few words. Often these were in the form of questions that demanded an instant response in order to release the mind from the world it had created and enable it to see things as they really are.

For example, the same woman may be seen as a wife by her husband, as a mistress by her lover, as a mother by her son, or as a grandmother by her grandchildren — but she is still only one woman. The interplay of mind and reality were brought to a state of enlightenment by the setting of riddles which the Zen priests called koans.

Meditation was an important part of the Zen Buddhist training. In silent contemplation the universe and the individual become one and the manacles of illusion give way to the enlightenment of reality once again. Step by step the world is experienced and seen as it really is and the illusions of the mind fade away forever.

The Zen philosophy of the samurai was known as Kamakura Zen and it was specifically directed to their needs and remained so throughout Japan's turbulent history. During the sixteenth century the famous Japanese swordsman Yagyu Sekishusai, who was influenced by the Zen priest Takuan, established a style called Yagyu Shinkage Ryu. This style reflected a change in philosophy as hitherto Zen training helped the warrior to find calm so that he could defeat his enemy in battle. Now killing in itself was not the objective; instead the emphasis was placed on finding Zen enlightenment through the training of the warrior.

Right: *A thorough understanding of natural law was of paramount importance in battle strategy.* **The Art of War** *by Sun Tzu advised on all strategic possibilities – whatever the terrain.*

The book of I-Ching

Zen training and the Zen mind developed the ideal state of being in which the warrior and martial arts exponent could function, but there were even more elemental aspects of the warrior philosophy that lay at the roots of natural phenomena. These were revealed in the early teachings of the legendary Chinese ruler Fu-hsi in the shape of trigrams which represented the relationship of opposites, the interrelationship of the five elements — wood, fire, earth, metal and water — and the universal harmony between man and nature. All these influences played a special part in the education of the warrior and martial arts exponent.

The trigrams of Fu-hsi were introduced to Japan in the seventh century and play a significant part in the warrior traditions. There are eight trigrams in total, all of which consist of three sets of lines. The broken line (yin) represents the negative principle of things and the unbroken line represents the positive principle (yang). The eight trigrams represent Creativity (positive), Yielding (negative), Beginning (thunder, earthquake), Trouble (digging a hole), Non-moving (completion), Gentle (peaceful), Discord (separation), Enticement (permeable). The trigrams are the components for the 64 hexagrams that make up the book of Yi-king (I-Ching), these 64 six-line structures being combinations of the eight trigrams (in the same way as in painting where all other colours derive from the primary colours). A later system by Wen Wang (1231-1135 BC) placed the same trigrams in a different order and meaning to Fu-hsi and used them for occult purposes, so it is important not to confuse the two concepts (see below).

In Japan the principles of yin and yang are known as in and yo, respectively. When the martial arts exponent understands the relationship of these opposites, he can apply the principles in his techniques. Let us look at strength and flexibility, for example, which are two opposites. By yielding to your opponent's strength, his force may be turned against him but if you are simply weak he will defeat you. If you use your strength against a weak opponent and yield if he becomes strong, you can again turn his strength to your advantage. If you can trick your opponent into believing that you will be strong, he will then respond with more strength than he needs and you can turn this against him. There is no end to the permutation of these concepts which spring from opposites. If, for example, you mix hot with cold you get warm in varying degrees depending on the mixture; or if you look for a balance between love and hate you will find indifference. Understanding the relationship of inyo (yinyang) and being able to apply its principles was one of the ingredients used by the warrior in the formulation of his strategy.

The I-Ching of Wen Wang was used particularly in fortune telling. This system, together with the principles of the five elements and the Chinese concepts of the order of the universe, constituted another philosophy brought to Japan around the seventh century. The principle of the order of things is as follows: There is one original existence that produced the duality of opposites called yin and yang. The result of this division is the creation of the universe, earth and man, motion in terms of space (represented by the four compass points) and in terms of time (represented by the four seasons), the five elements that control the pattern of life (water, earth, metal, fire, wood), and finally the six relationships which are ruler to subject, father to child and husband to wife.

The relationships of the five elements in symbolic terms show how their principles may be applied. Wood produces fire, fire produces earth (from the ashes), earth produces metal, metal produces water (iron ore is found near water and condensation gathers on cold metal), water produces wood (the trees feed from the moisture). The principles of the relationship between these elements are finite: wood defeats earth (the roots of the tree break up the earth), earth defeats water (by forming a barrier), water defeats fire (by extinguishing flames), fire defeats metal (by melting it), metal defeats wood (by cutting it, as with an axe).

The warrior used these principles in combat as well as for telling the future. An example of the use of the five elements in martial arts can be seen in the sword postures (called kamae) taken by the samurai prior to an encounter. In very early manuscripts describing samurai sword technique, there were three main stances: Ten where the sword was held above the head, Mizu with the sword held in middle position, and Chi with the sword in low position. Ten, Mizu and Chi represented heaven, water and earth, respectively. The strategy of the warrior was derived from elemental principles which developed into a complex study and interpretation of martial arts.

The esoteric elements of both the Chinese and Japanese fighting systems contained many magical formulae and were based on the principles described in this chapter. One of Japan's oldest martial traditions, Tenshin Shoden Katori Shinto Ryu, which dates back to the fourteenth century, used such techniques. Astrology, combined with the knowledge of natural law, was a means by which days of battle, places of encampment, the outcome of encounters and other devices of martial strategy were foretold. Talismen to protect the wearer were made by magical processes and the sites on which castles were built, which would be blessed with good luck, were also foretold by occult means.

The exponents of martial arts in the Far East looked into every facet of their skills, from cosmology to strategy, from philosophy to technique, uniting their technical powers with those of nature to produce the truly awe-inspiring martial skills of myth and history.

Right: *Warriors of both China and Japan studied the philosophies of the ancient sages to enhance their fighting ability.*

倍繩水滸傳豪傑百八人之一個

大刀關勝

蒲東郡れ産むつさる関将軍壽亭侯の蠣孫さり巡捨の職ぎ先祖關羽雲長もし相貌も黒うて然も紘青龍乃偃月刀を遺ふ東昌府の戦す十六人目ま打て出る張清が飛石を偃月刀そて請ふ勇を奮ふ

一勇齋 國芳画

Part of the 6,000-strong and lifesize terracotta army of Chinese emperor Huang Ti, surviving for over two thousand years.

3

THE CHINESE CONNECTION

The development of the Far Eastern martial arts has been overwhelmingly influenced by the history and culture of the Chinese nation in its many aspects. The early migrations — and even the later exodus of Chinese during the communist era — have led to their martial arts knowledge being spread across the entire Far East. Some of these martial skills have remained intact, whilst others have been influenced by the cultures of the people the Chinese have intermingled with. For instance, in Japan the early Chinese influence in martial arts has been a medium in which a completely independent martial culture has grown, and before we explore the pageant of Chinese history there are two important comparisons to be drawn between China and Japan.

The first is in the status of the warrior classes of both nations, whose social positions throughout history were completely opposite. The Japanese warrior enjoyed the privilege of being at the top of the social scale, which was reflected in the development of his fighting skills. However, after the fall of the noble warrior classes with the beginning of the Han dynasty in 206 BC, the Chinese warrior was not credited with the same status, either socially or intellectually.

The second comparison lies in the fact that many schools of martial arts in Japan kept records of both techniques and philosophy, considerable numbers of which have been passed down and survive to modern times as accurate historical records of the past. China's history is long and complicated and it is important to realize that every 'fact' is mixed with a little myth. Records of early times are sometimes misleading or inaccurate, or even non-existent in many aspects. This lack particularly applies to many records of martial arts, which were destroyed during the frequent razing of temples to the ground. Yet despite the gaping holes it is still possible to separate some myth from fact and build up a coherent picture of the Chinese connection in martial arts.

From the times of the gods

Although at times throughout history the Chinese nation has encompassed Manchuria, Mongolia and Tibet, China proper is a country surrounded by mountains, plateaus and deserts, with hot summers and cold winters in the north, while the south experiences long, hot, humid summers and rains and typhoons in the winter. The north and south are divided by a vast mountain range, and even the language is divided by many dialects. In the north Mandarin is spoken and in the area of Canton in the south the Cantonese dialect is used. There are many other dialects ranging between the two.

In Chapter 1 we introduced the divinity P'an ku who used his body to form the earth and mountains, his left eye becoming the sun and his right eye forming the moon. After him came Sui Jen, who introduced the skill of making fire. The legendary rulers Fu-hsi, Shen Nung and Tuang Ti introduced agricultural skills, as well as arts and crafts. The *pa-kua* (trigrams) were supposed to have been written on tortoise-shell by Fu-hsi. According to some historians the first real ruler was Huang Ti (the Yellow Emperor).

Weapons from early neolithic (6000 BC) Chinese cultures, axe heads and so forth, indicate links with other parts of the world at that time, but any concept of martial skill would amount to no more than primitive violence. There is also evidence that many early cultures in China believed in nature worship, which is often common in primitive agricultural man. The early farmer relied on the seasons and elements of nature to provide good conditions for his crops, so it was natural for religion and belief to grow in this way. It is certain that from these cults, the concepts of *yin* and *yang*, the harmony of nature and the universal forces, found their beginnings. One ritual encounter among the farming class involved the wearing of cow horns, the participants attacking and trying to gore each other, thus demonstrating a primitive union of religious belief and combative sportsmanship.

The dynasties begin

It was not until the period of the Shang and Chou dynasties (about 1500 to 221 BC) that written references provide us with some picture of those ancient times. During this period there were many small states that were governed by feudal lords, which were in turn protected by a clan system. A certain primitive code of chivalry existed, but with the lust for power and territory this soon declined. The chariot played a prominent part in battle strategy at this time, having been introduced from Central Asia during the thirteenth century BC. These vehicles were often used to intimidate the enemy and probably contained the charioteer, an archer and spearman. The rest of the troops were on foot and used the sword, dagger and spear. Some footsoldiers carried a crude sort of shield made of leather or woven bamboo but little is really known about the fighting techniques of the time.

The bow took a leading role in both warfare and sport during the Chou dynasty, along with music, their classics and writing. The nobles would indulge in competitions to show off their skills. One early story tells of a Chinese noble who displayed his skills by loosing one arrow after another, while balancing a glass of water on his head. A priest who was watching said to him 'this display is fine but it is not real archery; you impress the crowds but your skill is not complete'. The archer was indignant and challenged the priest to a match. The priest agreed, provided it was at his place of choosing — a spot high in the mountains. Once there, the priest suddenly sprang on to a narrow piece of rock reaching far out into the abyss below. With only an inch of rock beneath his feet, the priest called to the archer, 'quick, bring me the bow and I will loose an arrow into the void of this gorge'. The archer moved forward but as his feet touched the narrow ledge, he looked down at the sheer drop below and fell flat on the ground for safety. Then the priest said: 'in the face of death you cannot stand, let alone loose an arrow. How then can you call yourself a warrior?'

Left: *Gate of the temple of Confucius, Ching-hai, China. Confucius founded his philosophy on what he saw as the correct order of society and on the bonds of obligation.*

Above: *The Great Wall of China — an unbroken line of defence stretching over 2,250 km (1,400 miles) — was originally built to keep out Mongolian raiders.*

The age of the sage

Confucius (about 550-479 BC) was born in a land torn by war and anarchy. Fighting between barbarians on the borders of the Chinese territories and internal political struggles, together with the loose morals of the nobles, brought an age of discord and violence. Confucius was born in the state of Lu near Shantung and was a member of the Kung clan. He became a chief magistrate in his province but eventually resigned and wandered the country teaching his philosophy. He believed in the old codes of chivalry, the social and moral order of a cultured society and the integrity of its rulers. During this period none of the many philosophers, including Confucius or the Taoist scholar Lao Tzu, made any drastic changes to the decline of the era. (In fact, there is no real evidence for the historical existence of Lao Tzu. Many scholars attribute Taoism to the second-century Tao-ling.)

Towards the end of the Chou dynasty a new and irreversible trend in warfare developed. The chariot became obsolete, the cavalry being used as mounted archers backed up by footsoldiers. Around 400 BC strategy and tactics began to play an important role in warfare and combat and it was during this era that Sun Tzu, born in the area of Chi (modern-day Peking), wrote his manuscripts on *The Art of War*. During the lifetime of Sun Tzu the crossbow was developed and became a prominent weapon in warfare. Steel began to be used in battle; the works of Sun Tzu refer to steel-tipped lances being as sharp as bee stings.

About the time of Confucius' death the country fell into internal conflict which lasted for 250 years. Brigands roamed the marsh lands and desolate areas, there were many assassinations and other atrocities and despite the severity of the law, which included cutting off ears, noses and feet, lawlessness still prevailed. The Chou dynasty ended and gave way to the Ch'in in 221 BC. The founder of the Ch'in dynasty set himself up as 'The First Emperor' (Shi Huang Ti) and unified the country, dividing it into 36 states governed under his direction. Shi Huang Ti was ruthless in his administration, ordering the confiscation and destruction of all weapons not used by his armies. This act probably encouraged the growth of empty-hand fighting techniques and the use of everyday implements as weapons.

It was during Shi Huang Ti's reign that the Great Wall of China was built to prevent border attacks from Mongolian nomads and it covered a distance of 2,250 kilometres (1,400 miles). Shi Huang Ti also felt threatened from within — especially by propaganda spread by subdued noble families. The moral teachings of the earlier philosophers such as Confucius clearly showed the emperor as a tyrant and were used as a political vehicle for this purpose. As a result of this situation the most devastating event for historians took place: the burning of all learned books and historical records. Any scholar who was found concealing books or passing on the old teachings was put to death. Thus only a few books survived the Ch'in rule.

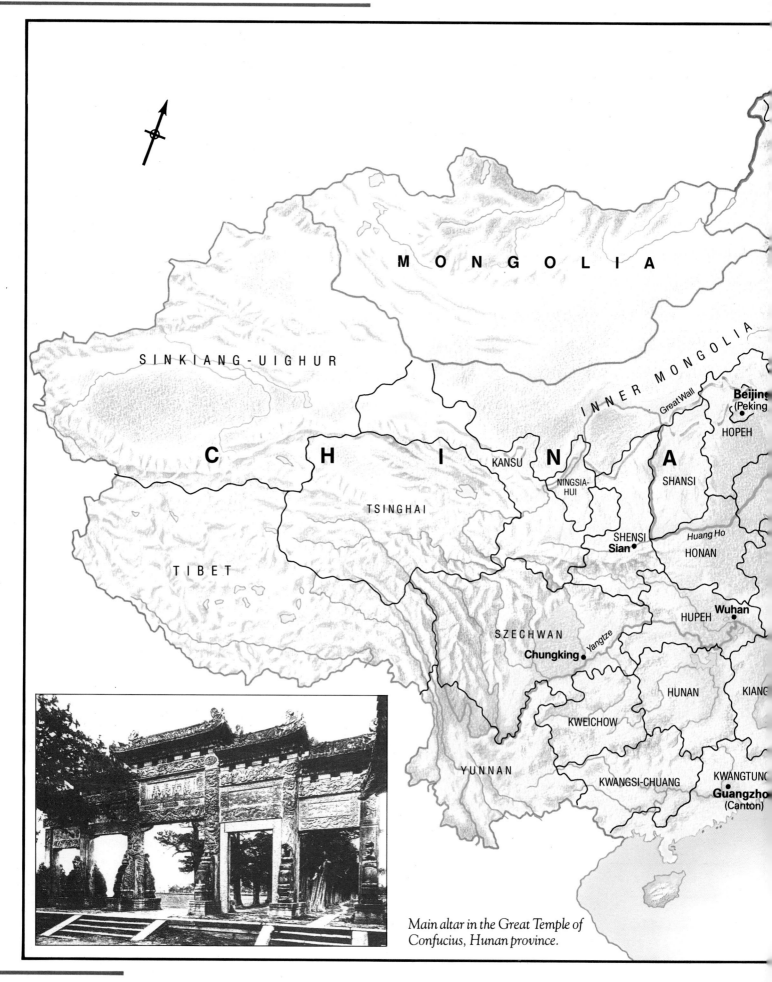

M O N G O L I A

SINKIANG-UIGHUR

INNER MONGOLIA

Great Wall

Beijing
(Peking)

HOPEH

C   H   I   N   A

KANSU

NINGSIA-HUI

SHANSI

TSINGHAI

SHENSI
Sian

Huang Ho

HONAN

TIBET

HUPEH   **Wuhan**

SZECHWAN
Yangtze

Chungking

HUNAN   KIANG

KWEICHOW

YUNNAN

KWANGSI-CHUANG

KWANGTUNG
Guangzho
(Canton)

*Main altar in the Great Temple of
Confucius, Hunan province.*

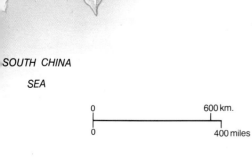

Chinese Historical Eras

Shang or Yin Kingdom	circa 1500-1100 BC
Early Chou Period	circa 1100- 722 BC
Ch'un Ch'iu Period	722- 481 BC
Period of the Warring States	481- 221 BC
Ch'in Dynasty	221- 206 BC
Han Dynasty	206 BC-AD 221
Three Kingdoms (San Kuo)	AD 221- 265
Tsin Dynasty	265- 316
Northern and Southern Empires (Nan Pei Chao)	316- 589
Sui Dynasty	589- 618
T'ang Dynasty	618- 907
Five Dynasty Period (Wu Tai)	907- 960
Sung Dynasty	960-1127
Kin and Southern Sung Dynasties	1127-1280
Yuan (Mongol) Dynasty	1280-1368
Ming Dynasty	1368-1644
Ch'ing (Manchu) Dynasty	1644-1911
Republic	1911-

Chapel in the rocks of the 1,000 Buddhas in Szechuan province.

The tides of change

On the death of Shi Huang Ti, fighting broke out for control of the country. In 206 BC Liu Pang, who came from peasant stock, founded the Han dynasty, which was an age of growth for both the warrior and scholar alike and lasted for all but a few of the next 400 years. With this new unity of China Liu Pang directed his armies at claiming new territories and resurrecting the remains of historical documents, hidden from the Ch'in dynasty. Confucianism became established and was revised to suit the country's needs. Taoism degenerated into a subcult for the magicians and alchemists; however, during their search for eternal life and the philosophers' stone, they inadvertently discovered gunpowder. One eminent surgeon of the time called Hua To studied Taoism and put its principles into effect. He devised a series of exercises based on the movements of five animals: bear, bird, deer, monkey and tiger.

By this period the skills of the soldier had fallen to the commoners and nobles alike, both fighting side by side. The 'chun tzu', who had been the warrior ruling class, much like the samurai of the later period in Japan, ceased to retain that status and in order for the emperor to retain his position the social structure according to Confucius was strongly emphasized, with loyalty and obedience beginning with the ruler. In this era reference was made to fighting skills in both the *Han Book of Arts* and the *Shou Po*, a work that dealt with empty-hand fighting and which also contained 38 chapters on the use of the sword. Although both of these works have since been lost, we do know that both swords and halberds were standard weapons of the period and that footsoldiers used spears that had a bladed protrusion from the side to allow both thrusting and cutting actions in battle.

First secret societies

The Han dynasty explored new territories and formed contacts with the Western world. The culture of China spread as far as Japan, knowledge of Buddhism came from India and trade grew with other nations. The first secret societies began to appear, organizations with their members skilled in martial arts, with religious and often cult backgrounds. The first of these were the Red Eyebrows, a society that rebelled against the emperor Kuang Wu Ti after his ascension to the throne in AD 25. Towards the end of the Han dynasty another more feared secret society called the Yellow Turbans tipped the scales of power. This group was believed to be invincible and to have supernatural powers, which were obtained through mystical rites. As a direct result of their rebellion the Han dynasty collapsed.

With the fall of the Han dynasty in AD 221 the country was divided into three states and the nation once again fell into anarchy for about the next 400 years. There were many invasions from the Tartar and other bordering nations who adopted much of the Chinese culture. It was during this time, in AD 339, that the monk Fa Hsien made his journey to India across the Hindu Kush, to collect the Buddhist scriptures. After 15 years he returned to China by sea, spending the rest of his life translating the scriptures. In about AD 520 Bodhidarma (Tamo in Chinese) founded the Ch'an (Zen in Japanese) school of Buddhism in China and according to tradition Bodhidarma introduced fighting skills to the monks at the Shaolin temple in Honan. In reality there is little evidence to substantiate any of these claims.

We only know that Bodhidarma did exist (possibly he was Persian or Indian) and did go to China. It could possibly be that he was the first Buddhist to introduce fighting skills to his monks, but not the first time that monks had studied fighting skills. Buddhism and Taoism flourished as the warriors' skills developed through these violent epochs.

Sui and T'ang dynasties lasted from about 589 to 907. This was a time when the first leaves of Shaolin martial arts began to grow and the precepts of tai-chi were consolidated. New contacts were made with the Western world and many ideas about Chinese culture were taken back to Japan by visiting emissaries. The doors to India opened even further and the travelling scholar Hsuan Tsang returned from India with some 600 volumes of Buddhist texts and retreated to the Shaolin temple in Honan.

The somewhat fragmented nation was once again united by Li Shi Min, who became the first T'ang emperor in about 618. He called upon the assistance of the Shaolin temple in Honan (which was built by the emperor Hsiao Wen (386-557) to defeat his adversary Wang She Tsung. He was so impressed by the ability of the thirteen fighting monks that assisted him, that he gave permission for 500 warriors to be trained there. In 845 a decree was passed by another T'ang emperor to ban Buddhism, resulting in many temples being destroyed. In 887, however, his successor, who favoured Buddhism, repealed this decree.

When the T'ang dynasty ended there were 50 years of more confusion and anarchy until in 960 China was again unified under the Sung emperors. This was an age of great cultural development. Chu Hsi gave a new perspective to Confucianism that in time became recognized and accepted as the orthodox form. This philosophy was, however, influenced by the *I-Ching* which, as described in Chapter 2, contains the trigrams, hexagrams and interpretations. Against this background of philosophical influences various concepts of Chinese boxing began to develop.

Tradition relates that Chang San-feng introduced a style of boxing that was defensive in nature and based on Taoist principles. This idea of yielding and defensive techniques became known as the internal system, an example of this being tai-chi. The hard offensive systems are expressed as positive and powerful and can be seen in styles like Shaolin Ch'uan. Both internal and external systems existed in the Sung dynasty and it was an era in which Chinese boxing grew as a matter of necessity, encouraged by the success of the Shaolin temple in Honan.

Above right: *The Shaolin monk Haideng is both a master of wu-shu and the abbot of the Shaolin monastery in Henan province.*

Right: *The burial place of senior monks of the Shaolin temple.*

Mongol rule

Between 1260 and 1368 China was ruled by the conquering Mongols, having first been crushed at Peking by the ruthless Genghis Khan. Kublai Khan established his rule in 1260 after the death of Ghengis Khan, and set up his capital in Peking. The great explorer Marco Polo, who served Kublai for many years, brought word of this new Chinese empire to Europe and by 1249 there was a growing Christian community, together with other missionaries, in China. Kublai sent an invading force to Japan during his rule, but this was perhaps his greatest disaster, as his extensive fleet was totally destroyed.

Towards the end of the Mongol rule, oppression drove the Chinese into revolt. Chu Yuan-chang was born a peasant of those times in the Huai area of southern China. When he was still a boy he joined a Buddhist monastery and studied the martial skills, but because of the troubled times he left the order and formed a large group of rebels from former bandits. Chu Yuan-chang then sought the support of the secret society called the White Lotus and with their help took control of Nanking, which became his capital. He drove out the Mongol invaders and by 1368 he had become emperor and founded the Ming dynasty.

By the third Ming emperor Yung Lo the capital had moved to Peking in northern China. Peking was rebuilt and the Great Wall strengthened, but the nation was in constant strife due to border invaders and Japanese pirates. When Japan attacked Korea in 1592, the Chinese gave support, which further weakened their defences. Eventually internal rebellion weakened the Ming dynasty and it fell to the Manchus in 1644.

Above: *The dramatic legends of the Shaolin temples and their warriors are still popular today — especially with cinema audiences.*

Right: *This contemporary illustration of the Boxer Rebellion shows the violence and destruction of the doomed uprising.*

The Manchurian conquest

In 1644 Li Tzu-ch'eng, the leader of a rebel Chinese group, took control of Peking, the last Ming emperor taking his own life rather than face capture. However, not everyone accepted the rule of Li Tzu-ch'eng; one of his major adversaries was Wu San-kuei who held a grudge against the ruler for stealing his wife. During a battle between the two arch enemies, Wu San-kuei drove his adversary further and further west, until he finally defeated him. While this personal vendetta was in progress, Peking was unguarded and easily fell to the Manchus from the north who founded the Ch'ing dynasty which lasted until 1911.

Manchu power did not, however, extend to the south; there a Ming prince still remained to claim his heritage. Wu San-kuei, who had studied the skills of the Chinese Boxers, sought the backing of the Manchu court in Peking and the awesome power of the White Lotus Society, to defeat the Ming power in the southern capital of Nanking. Some traditions hold that there was a second Shaolin temple in the southern province of Fukien and that 128 Shaolin fighting monks were deployed to assist Wu San-kuei, by demonstrating their usual invincible skills. After the flight of the Ming prince, it is said that the Manchus razed this temple to the ground because they feared its power. The truth of this had never been substantiated but it is known that Wu San-kuei did turn against Manchu rule and in 1673 a great rebellion took place against the northern ruler K'ang Hsi. The outcome was a divided nation of north and south. After the death of Wu San-kuei the Manchus eventually took control of the southern territories.

The nation remained divided in spirit, the south with its capital at Nanking and the north at Peking. In the south there was great hatred towards the Manchurians and a greater tendency to retain more of the old cultures. The White Lotus secret society of the Boxers stimulated Manchu hatred and many other secret Boxer organizations began to grow in the south, as well as in the north. Christian missionaries continued to spread the word of their God but Western trade was limited by impositions from the Manchu court. Corruption among Manchu officials led to a mass illegal trade in opium from India which adversely affected the economy. Eventually, in the 1850s, the hate of the White Lotus Society for Manchurians and foreigners erupted in a violent struggle known as the T'ai P'ing rebellion. The movement was started by a dissident called Hung Hsiu-ch'uan who had a curious background of Protestant and Chinese religious education. He saw his destiny in a vision during a severe illness. The rebellion began in Kwangsi and moved north. The rebels captured Nanking in the south but were halted almost at the doors of Peking itself. Hung Hsiu-ch'uan ruled southern China from Nanking for almost nine years, while the Manchu continued their reign in the north. Eventually a Chinese army, led by George Gordon, an English major, defeated the rebels and restored order for the Manchu rule. However the price was high and foreign power began to take more control of China.

The Boxer Rebellion and its aftermath

By now there were many secret societies who claimed their descent from earlier organizations such as the White Lotus. All of them hated the Manchu rule, all foreigners and Christianity. One of the more powerful of these sects was the I Ho Chuan (Fist of Righteous Harmony), but there were many others such as the Red Spear, Big Swords and Eight Diagram sect. Shantung was the centre of their growth, their teachings flourishing on esoteric Buddhism and the mystic rites of Taoism. Although these groups — the forerunners of the modern Triad organizations — took the limelight during the period leading up to the Boxer Rebellion in 1900, there were many masters of empty-hand and weapon skills during this era who passed on martial arts traditions of the past without recourse to secret organizations or political intrigue.

In 1894 Japan declared war on China and by March 1895 China had capitulated and signed the treaty of Shimonoseki. Manchu power was broken, but the territory gained by Japan was divided by the pressure of Western intervention. Britain leased Hong Kong, the United States took Hawaii, Germany leased Tsingtau and France had Kwangchow bay. Tzun Hsi, the Empress Dowager, came to the throne and the scene was set for the Boxer Rebellion.

As the Chinese became more and more aware of the exploitation of their nation by foreigners, conflict grew between Christianity and the ethnic religions. A smouldering hatred permeated Chinese society, which was 'brushed under the carpet' by the Western powers. The Boxers began to gain public favour by giving demonstrations of their 'invincibility'. In public

they performed amazing feats, showing apparent invulnerability to the gun, sword and knife. These incredible feats were attained by self-induced trances, fanatical beliefs, drugs, and often trickery. There were, of course, failures. One disciple was spread across a very wide area by a cannon ball he failed to stop — his vulnerability being attributed to his lack of faith.

Many Chinese joined the movement, which grew rapidly in the northeast, and it soon became clear that even the Empress Dowager was turning a blind eye, if not condoning their actions. A main target were Chinese Christians, who often had their ears and noses cut off or their eyes gouged, before being put to death. At Taiyuan in the Shansi province on 9 July 1900 over 40 foreigners were beheaded on the order of the Chinese governor, among them women and children.

On 17 June 1900 Peking was under siege by the Boxers backed by Chinese soldiers. The Boxers, who wore red bands around their hair, wrists and ankles, looked an awesome sight in their white costumes with red sashes around their waists. The siege was long and bloody, and eventually the foreigners and diplomats took refuge in the British legation. As weeks went by the stench of rotting bodies outside the legation, and the smell from unsanitary conditions within, filled the air. By 14 August, in the face of almost certain defeat, an international European force took control of Peking and ended the siege. The Empress Dowager fled and the Boxer uprising crumbled.

When the Empress Dowager died in 1908 the Manchu rule fell apart and ended in 1912 when the boy emperor Pu Yi abdicated in favour of a republic. After World War I communism began to grow. Despite some Japanese intervention, in 1928 under Chiang Kai-shek the communists took control of Peking. In 1937 war broke out between China and Japan which was compounded by the events of World War II. With the defeat of Japan and other internal events, the Chinese People's Republic was established in 1949. Martial skills were initially restricted after 1949 but there has been a resurgence of interest since the Cultural Revolution of the 1960s.

Opposite above: Running parallel with the tranquil contemplation of the philosophers, was a subcult of violence that culminated in the Boxer Rebellion, incited by the Empress Dowager Tzun Hsi.

Opposite below: Violent conflict was endemic in China at the time of the Boxer Rebellion — including clashes at the Russian border.

Below: Myths of Boxer invincibility were soon dispelled when thousands of rebels were put to the sword at the climax of the rebellion.

Millennia of martial arts

When looking at the events of Chinese history that are concerned with the development of martial skills, we must make allowances for speculation where documentation does not exist. No doubt the early fighting monks learned weapon systems from skilled warriors, masters of weapons who were renowned for their ability. So it seems obvious that the weapon skills of the early Chinese warrior and the empty-hand systems of the monks have merged into compatibility. Thus the weapons of any true Chinese traditional style should and do blend in with its empty-hand systems.

Throughout history there was a division of thought between the occult and the natural aspects of martial arts philosophy. There was also a difference in martial arts styles between southern and northern China, which was partly due to custom, clothing and climate.

Not all Boxers were martial arts exponents and not all martial arts exponents were Boxers. It was not uncommon for a master of such skills to seek the solitude of a temple or mountain retreat, where his closeness to nature touched the very heart of true Taoist teachings. Many styles grew because of the prowess of a teacher in war or in personal encounters; as the reputation of the school was enhanced so it was passed down to modern times.

The bloody and confused history of China itself has been the nutriment for the unusual growth of hundreds of different fighting styles, with only the most enduring having survived. Some of these supreme fighting styles will be described in the next chapter.

Left: *The ancient tourist attractions of modern China bear silent witness to the bloody pages of Chinese history that were a testing ground for the martial arts.*

Below: *The Three Pure Ones of the Taoist trinity. The concepts of Taoism are based on man's efforts to find harmony with the universal forces of nature through meditation.*

In the Songshan mountains of Henan province,
master Yang Jucai, teacher of Shaolin boxing,
exercises in front of a Shaolin temple.

4

CHINESE STYLES

The term 'kung-fu' is perhaps the most popular Western expression used to describe the Chinese martial arts. This expression is, however, very misleading as 'kung-fu' is in fact a Cantonese word merely meaning 'an acquired skill'. It can refer equally to knitting or cookery as it can to the martial arts! The one word that the Chinese themselves use to describe their martial arts is *wu-shu*, a mandarin term describing the collective study of martial skills.

The illusion of mystery

Many people who have not trained in the martial arts — and others who have only trained to a small degree — believe that miracles and magic can be performed by true exponents of the skills. A small child, watching a conjuror making coins appear from thin air and from behind people's ears, believes that such things are really possible — as if by magic. One day, as a mature person and knowing the truth, he will watch another conjuror perform the same coin trick. For the first time he will realize just how much skill is required to make the trick look like magic.

The same applies to the martial arts. Any true skill looks effortless in the hands of a master and the perfect execution of a technique appears almost as if performed by magic. However, the master's secrets lie in the knowledge of both natural and physical laws, that may be expressed in both intellectual and intuitive understanding. Through his knowledge and skills, the mind, body and spirit are united and become one with the universe. This is the way of the masters of martial arts — and of other great artists in their own particular fields.

What the Chinese people saw and marvelled at during the Boxer Rebellion may have been the skilful use of martial arts — or pure illusion. Two examples from the author's own experience well illustrate the difference, where in both cases a piece of 2.5cm (1 inch) pine board was split using only the fingers of a thrusting hand. In the first case the exponent was skilful and during his years of training he had conditioned his hand to withstand the pain by building up a thick wall of hard skin on the fingertips. When he thrust at the board and split it in two, his balance was excellent and he used the total application of leverage and concentrated force, making the feat seem effortless and almost magical. In the second case, when the author had the opportunity to look at the board before it was broken, he found that it had been placed in an oven to dry out, making it extremely brittle and vulnerable to the slightest touch. This 'exponent' included much theatrical build-up in his display, including leaping about and shouting.

Right: *Both the movements and spirit of animals and birds were captured by Chinese masters of wu-shu and embodied in their martial arts training.*

Far right: *Master Liu Zhiqing, leader of the Wushu Association of Harbin in northern China. Since the Cultural Revolution there has been a resurgence of interest in martial arts in China.*

When he broke the board his balance was very bad and his energy was lost in all directions. Ironically, both exponents received equally ecstatic applause from their audiences, who saw only the final effect and not the skill of the one true exponent.

The first rule is that genuine martial arts are based on truth. To understand this you must separate the truth from the illusion, which is also found in the teaching of Buddhism.

The styles and their features

The Chinese martial arts are divided broadly into northern and southern styles. There are 'soft' and 'hard' styles, which can be 'internal' or 'external'. There are also forms which contain a little of both. We do not have the space here to discuss all the many hundreds of systems that exist in China, but we can outline the basic principles and describe the more prominent schools.

Northern and southern styles differ quite considerably, which is partly due to differences in geography between northern and southern China, and partly to differences in culture and traditions. Northerners are often bigger in stature than southerners and have strong legs, no doubt due to the many mountainous regions of their terrain. In the agricultural south the inhabitants are of slighter build and use their hands more in their work. There are also many other inherent factors that account for the southern style's predominant use of hands in fighting and the

northern style's use of feet. Generally, northern styles employ large movements with jumping kicks, while southern styles are more firmly based on the ground. The northern schools practise in prearranged sequences of technique, while southern schools encourage sparring in their training curriculum.

Soft and hard styles are the outward manifestations of training principles. The easiest way to understand the division between the two is to contrast the use of a bow and a spear. The archer nocks the arrow to the bow string, which yields to the arrow as it is pulled back. Then that energy is released and returned to the arrow so that it penetrates its target. This can be equated with the soft styles. On the other hand, the man with the spear runs into battle holding the spear close to his body and as he runs the point penetrates its target. The power of the thrust is initiated from his own strength, there is no yielding and returning: it is a hard technique. Thus hard finds a direct route and forces its will using strength and power, while soft yields to the force and turns it to its advantage.

Internal and external styles express the differences in both training and application of techniques. External styles condition the body, develop physical power and take the outward manifestations of strength. Internal styles develop inward body functions, such as breathing, intuitive response and strength of will, and outwardly appear yielding and flowing.

Far left: *Bruce Lee, although contributing almost singlehandedly to the popularizing of the martial arts in the West, nevertheless portrayed an image of the ancient fighting skills which contrasts with the stoic ideals of the classical masters.*

Left: *The flowing movements of tai-chi are built on a foundation of complete stability; the posture and body lines are strong whilst the movements are as yielding as a willow branch.*

The hard styles and the Shaolin temple

The hard styles stem from the Shaolin temple in the northern Sung mountains of Honan and perhaps at a later date were introduced to the southern Shaolin temple in the Fukien area — however, there is little hard historical evidence to substantiate this story. The first fighting exercises from the northern temple were attributed to Bodhidarma (Tamo in Chinese) around AD 520 and consisted of 18 fighting postures known as the Lohan system. Later the first Sung emperor Chao Kuang-yin (960-976) introduced another 32 forms called 'long boxing' to complement the Lohan system. Just before the Ming dynasty, a monk called Chueh Yuan restyled the system to include a total of 72 techniques and it is claimed that at a later date Pai Yu Feng formulated the system into its present form with a total of 170 techniques.

Shaolin techniques are founded on the movements of five animals: the dragon, tiger, snake, leopard and crane. However, it is unlikely that these forms originated from actual techniques used by these animals — certainly not the dragon! A more likely explanation is that Hua T'o, a doctor of the Han dynasty, used exercises based on animal movement to promote health, and it is probable that such parallels were used to convey the feeling required to execute the respective techniques.

According to legend, only five Shaolin monks survived the burning of the temples during the Manchu rule and after their escape they spread the teachings of Shaolin throughout the country. It is probable that many more escaped the devastation, but there is little evidence left of the times and their events. What

is a fact is that the hard styles of the Shaolin monks did eventually split into two divisions, following the different concepts of north and south.

The soft way of Taoism

While the Shaolin styles are founded on Buddhist philosophy, the internal styles are founded on Taoism. One theory concerns Chang San-feng who lived during the period of Mongol rule (1260-1368) and was born in the Hupei area of central China. This Taoist priest developed a system of defensive boxing which was a forerunner of tai-chi. Its principles are based on the *yin-yang*, the five elements and the concepts of the *pa-kua* (trigrams).

One important aspect of such training is the existence of *chi* (*ki* in Japanese), which is the universal energy that exists in all things. A true understanding of breathing is the cornerstone of the internal systems, because correct breathing fills the body with this life force. At the moment of death the last breath leaves the body; with the first cry of a newborn child the intake of air gives it independent life. How we breathe affects our well being and our health and plays a most important but subliminal part in our life.

The concept called *prana* by the exponents of Yoga also reflects the life force of *chi*; this is not breath itself but the life force it brings with it. The singer, for example, fills the lungs with air by expanding the chest, which allows greater resonance. The wrestler takes air into the lungs but expands the diaphragm instead, in this way retaining greater stability and strength. The outlet of air during stress is important. If someone lifts a heavy object they often exclaim 'aagh' or 'huu' at the point of maximum exertion, which gives them that little extra strength. Fear is accompanied by shallow irregular breathing, surprise by a sudden intake of breath; if correct breathing techniques are used at these moments of stress then these emotions can be controlled.

The internal benefits of tai-chi

The internal martial arts styles each have their own source of origin. Tai-chi, for example, is a means to health, a martial art and a meditative practice. In China today it can be seen practised by millions in parks and other open spaces, by young and old alike. However, the slow, graceful, sweeping movements hide a more subtle and powerful defensive system. At some time during the Manchu rule, Wang Tsung-yueh introduced tai-chi into the Honan province, but from that time until now there have been many divisions. There were originally 13 postures and five foot movements which represented the trigrams and the five elements. At first the forms are practised alone, but later a partner is included. Although the movements are yielding and the exponents flexible, a subtle inner iron-like strength is required by experienced exponents.

An example of a tai-chi master's inner strength was recalled by the late Donn Draeger, who was without doubt the world's greatest Western authority on martial arts. Just after World War II Draeger's guest at his flat in Japan was a renowned tai-chi master. One day his privacy at home was rudely interrupted by a group of high-grade exponents of aikido who wanted to see what his guest was made of. The tai-chi master, showing no signs of annoyance, asked one of the stronger men to apply any lock he liked to him. While the exponent was trying his powerful technique, the tai-chi master simply placed his hand on the exponent's shoulder and without any effort, gently and gradually pushed him flat on the ground. This story not only reflects the power of tai-chi, it also amply demonstrates that rudeness and the show of ego do not go hand in hand with the true spirit of martial arts.

The style of hsing-i

Another northern style called hsing-i is an internal system attributed to Yueh Fei during the late Sung dynasty. While there is no concrete proof that this is the case, the tenth to twelfth centuries do seem to have been a period of growth for the Taoist martial skills. Perhaps like Chan San-feng with tai-chi, the early concepts of hsing-i sprang from Yueh Fei. One of the earliest recorded masters of hsing-i is Chi Lung-feng who was born during the Ming dynasty and learned the art from a Taoist priest in the Shansi area. Eventually the style divided into two schools, one of which was the original Shansi and the other Honan.

Hsing-i is more linear in appearance than tai-chi, but Taoist principles pervade the system. The five forms of attack are based on the principles of the five elements and their interrelationship, while the twelve sequences of movement are based on the principles of twelve animals. The concepts of yin and yang are expressed in the ideals of emptiness and fullness: from the meditative state of emptiness the spontaneous response to any situation is possible.

The internal power of pa-kua

The third style of the internal systems is called pa-kua, which can be traced to the central coastal province of Kiangsu. As with the other two styles, according to legend a Taoist priest living in the mountain regions passed his knowledge on to Tung Hai-ch'uan, who lived in the Ch'ing dynasty of Manchu rule. During his lifetime he revealed his skills to only a few students, but nevertheless left behind a healthy reputation. One day he was attacked by numerous armed assailants and defeated them without sustaining even the slightest injury. There have been many great pa-kua masters throughout history down to modern times. One of these, Ch'eng T'ing-hua, fought in the Boxer Rebellion. Legend has it that he was cornered by a large number of soldiers and despatched over twelve of them single-handed.

*Three of China's leading **wu-shu** champions in action. Their skills encompass a wide variety of weapon and empty-hand techniques.*

The system of pa-kua is founded on the eight trigrams and the teachings from the *I-Ching*. The attributes of each trigram (rather than their literal translation) are as follows: *ch'ien* is strong, *tui* is joyful, *li* is light-giving, *chan* is inciting movement, *sun* is penetrating, *k'an* is dangerous, *kan* is resting, *kw'un* is yielding. The techniques are performed in a circling movement although the actual actions employ horizontal power. The exponent moves around the circle adopting various techniques based on the above philosophy. The exponent looks like a wildcat that is being stalked by a dog. The dog makes a wide circle around the wildcat, who keeps turning to face the dog thus protecting his circular territory. The dog springs in but the wildcat fights him back at each point as he attempts to enter the circle, the wildcat's territory remaining the central pivot for the defensive action.

Hard styles of north and south

The external systems of hard boxing use the five animal forms of the dragon, snake, tiger, leopard and crane. Each creature expresses a character of its own which conveys an idea and feeling for training in that form. The dragon develops and unites inner spirit, the snake improves the *chi*, and both forms accommodate grappling movements. The tiger strengthens the bones and the leopard develops strength, both of these forms using powerful offensive tactics. There are various forms of tiger style, known as white, red and black. One example is the Shantung Black Tiger Style, which originated from Pai in Honan and portrays the strong vigorous movements extremely well. The crane conveys vitality, is defensive and retaliates with fast counter-attacks.

In the north are several variations to these hard styles, such as t'ang-lang which is an exception and based on the movements of the praying mantis. The founding of the style is attributed to Wang Lang who lived about 300 years ago in Shantung. It is said that he developed the style by adding the footwork of the monkey to the mantis hand techniques.

Wing-chun is a southern system based on straight-line punching, one special feature being chi-sau which involves constant contact with the attacker's hands. This style is attributed to Yim Wing-chun who studied under Ng Mui, a nun from the northern Shaolin temple. This style came down to modern times in the hands of master Yip Man, who included among his students the legendary Bruce Lee.

Shaolin temple: fact and fiction

In southern China there are purported to be five main hard styles from the Shaolin tradition named after their founders. These are called Hung, Ts'ai, Li, Mo and Liu. In fact there are now numerous external styles that claim their roots from the original Shaolin temple. The word *shaolin* means 'young forest' (in Cantonese it is pronounced *siu-lum* and in Japanese *shorin-ji*), but the reason it was chosen to symbolize the source of the Chinese boxing tradition rests deep in the past and its legends.

At the gates of the original Shaolin temple, hidden in the mists of the Sung mountain area of Honan, would-be students endured all the elements, waiting for months to be accepted by the mystic and powerful masters. Once admitted they encountered the labyrinth of passages that led to gruelling test after test. During many years of degradation and suffering, powers beyond the realms of man and gods were revealed to them. At last, after lifting the final stone urn of burning embers,

the mark of the temple was burned forever upon their arms and they entered the outside world once again. Moulded and reborn in the figure of a Shaolin master, the years of training now weighed lightly on their invincible frames and with their ethereal bodies they could even penetrate walls and vanish at will from the sight of their attackers.

The more accurate truth probably lies in human nature and man's urge to mythologise. Many came to the Shaolin temple for short durations of training, including perhaps warriors who wished to enhance their skills in battle. The monks were both dedicated to Buddhism and martial arts training, through which their beliefs were perpetuated. Their personal training, influenced by the natural environment in which they lived, was no doubt very gruelling and because of the intensity of their study and search for perfection, their abilities seemed almost magical. These circumstances, together with stories of their valour, told and retold over the centuries, have no doubt led to much over-exaggeration. Many disciples, who came to train, probably gave up and left of their own free will when things got tough. The few who stayed were probably taken into the confidence of the masters for more in-depth training and eventually became masters themselves.

Below: *At break of day on the streets of Shanghai, people of all ages practise the healthy art of tai-chi before starting the day's work.*

*Liang Yiquan, a Shaolin master, uses the **ch'iang**
(spear) as if it were a natural extension of his body.*

5

CHINESE WEAPONS

Chinese weapons are both apart from and a part of the martial arts of China. This dichotomy can easily be explained, because the warrior used arms from early times, while the Buddhist monks, from which Chinese boxing developed, forbade the use of weapons. The Shaolin monks of Zen Buddhism used only their hands, but as time went on the priest's staff and other religious objects were sometimes used for defence. However, it is not known when empty-hand systems took weapons into their repertoire. Over the centuries skilful warriors came to train in both Taoist and Buddhist empty-hand skills. Sometimes these warriors adopted and adapted the empty-hand skills or introduced their weapon skills into styles not bound by religion.

Over a period of time, some empty-hand styles developed their own fighting techniques with weapons and today weapon skills and empty-hand techniques are united in many Chinese martial arts. Unlike Japanese martial arts, the Chinese empty-hand forms are invariably taught to students first, then after years of training, weapons are introduced into the curriculum. The classical schools of the Japanese warrior always taught the weapons styles first. Once these skills had been mastered, the empty-hand techniques would be introduced.

In the Shang and Chou dynasties the spear, straight sword and spear-shaped dagger were used in battle. Most early weapons were made of bronze and many ceremonial weapons were made from jade and inset with precious jewels. Although iron was available from before 500 BC, the big step forward came with the introduction of steel. The traditional story is that Kan Chiang and his wife Mo Yeh forged a magnificent sword for the king of Wu in about 300 BC and as more smiths discovered the secret, the craft of forging steel weapons grew. With steel blades the arts of the warrior began to develop and many weapons entered their arsenals.

Chinese martial arts weapons can be divided into two groups: those introduced for the warrior and those developed by ordinary citizens simply for protection. The latter were often farm implements such as pitchforks and hoes, while warrior weapons included the *chien* (straight sword), *tao* (curved broadsword), *piao* (short dagger), *ch'iang* (spear), *san cha* (trident), *kung pang* (long pole), *kwan tao* (similar to a halberd), *cha* (pronged truncheon) and *san chet kwon* (three-sectional staff). Other weapons included the butterfly knives, axe, chain whip, iron club and of course the bow and arrow. Each weapon is compatible with the empty-hand system in which it is used.

Both the internal and external styles employ weapon forms. One master of hsing-i, Kuo Yun-shen, was a master of sword and spear, while in tai-chi sword and spear are

again traditional weapons. The techniques of the *chien* (straight sword) have been documented as far back as the Han dynasty and in the Shaolin styles portray very powerful and dynamic movements, while in contrast the internal forms such as tai-chi display an almost dance-like quality of flowing and sweeping movements.

The *chien* (straight sword)

The primary weapon of the warrior was perhaps the *chien* or straight sword which was used particularly for thrusting and also for slashing and cutting. Since the mythical forging of swords by Kan Chiang there has been the belief in the spirit of the sword and in the Chou period sword guards were ornamented with religious symbols to protect the owner and give him the power of victory. Even bronze swords from about 100 BC have been found with such amulets of protection upon them. One tradition holds that the sword must not be brought directly over the head in case it inhibits the area of the fontanel which itself is sword-shaped and has a spiritual significance.

Many great warriors through China's history have been renowned for their sword skills. For example the first Sung emperor Chao Kuang-yin was purported to have been a master of weaponry before entering the Shaolin temple. The first T'ang emperor T'ang T'ai Tsung not only used his sword skills to bring unity to his era but also recognized the merits of the pen to administer his dynasty. Many generals were also famous boxers and skilled in the weapon arts.

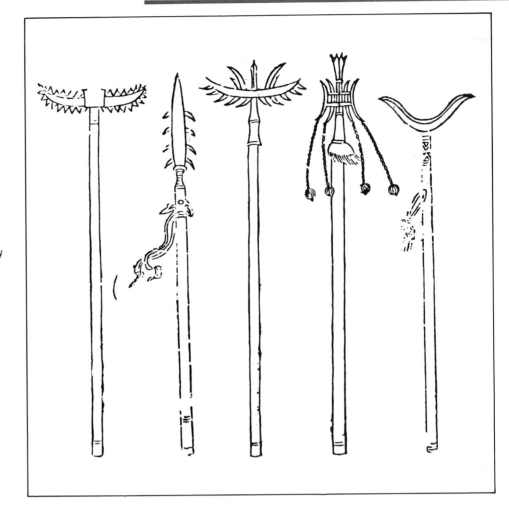

Far left: *Weapons, including the* **kwan tao** *(halberd), were always compatible with the empty-hand forms with which they developed.*

Left: *The* **chien** *(straight sword) is used by many Chinese styles. This exponent is imitating the praying mantis.*

Below left: *Sword guards were decorated with amulets for power and protection against any foe — human or demonic.*

Right: *The designs of many early Chinese weapons were as complex as they were intricate and varied.*

Below right: *The mounted warrior made full use of the stirrup (invented in China) so that both hands were free to wield his weapon in combat.*

The *ch'iang* (spear)

The *ch'iang* is almost as old as warfare itself. The Chinese spear was not a throwing weapon and in early times the shaft was very long, which made it ideal for the battlefield, where it was often employed in the front line. Its length kept the enemy at a distance, preventing the penetration of the ranks. In later years more personal encounters saw the development of a shorter shaft of about 2.7 metres (9 ft) in length. The shaft of the spear was made of hard wood which allowed a certain amount of flexibility. The spearheads of the early periods were made of bronze and later of steel. At the joining of the spear to the shaft the shaft goes into the spear socket. In fact early Japanese spears were mounted in this fashion and were called *hoko*. Later Japanese designs saw the tang of the spear inserted into the shaft, which again indicates the early Chinese influence in Japanese martial skills. The Chinese spear had a thick red tassel attached to the area of the shaft and spear joint. This was usually made of horsehair and part of its original purpose was to prevent blood from running down the shaft.

The spear is primarily a thrusting weapon, with the shaft being used to block and deflect any counter-attacks. In the Chinese forms, thrusts are often made using the full length of the shaft, allowing both hands to retreat to the end, while making the forwards thrusting movement. The founder of hsing-i, Chi Lung Feng, was said to be an excellent master of the spear before he learned his boxing skills from a priest in the Chung-nan mountains in central China.

Opposite: *The skills of the multi-edged weapon called a **yue** are still practised by wu-shu masters today in China.*

Above left: *Age is no barrier to perfection of skill; in pair-form training perfect judgement must be executed. Here two Chinese masters work in harmony together with broadswords.*

Below left: *The staff is a universal weapon and in China even the very young forge their character through its disciplined training.*

The *piao* (short dagger)

The *piao* is a short dagger which has been carried by the warrior since early times. This weapon can be traced back long before the Han dynasty and resembles a spearhead with a handle. Early forms of this weapon have been found carved in jade, but it is probable that the weapons used in combat were made of bronze. The present-day weapon is made of steel and apart from being used in close combat for thrusting and stabbing, it is also thrown. Very little is known of the early techniques but the *piao* has become part of the arsenal of classical Chinese weaponry.

The *kwan tao* (halberd)

Another early weapon that was popular on the battlefield is the *kwan tao*. This halberd-type weapon dates from before the Han dynasty. However, although like the spear its design has changed through the centuries, in essence the principles of its form and use have remained the same. The *kwan tao* has a curved blade which is attached in the same manner as the spear to a long shaft. The technique for its use includes many sweeping and slicing actions. This was an excellent weapon for use against the cavalry during China's early history.

The *tao* (broadsword)

The *tao* resembles the Western cutlass, but it has a double curved blade in the shape of a shallow 'S'. The hilt does not have the guard of a cutlass, instead there is a thick oval tray-like guard. The weapon is about 1 metre (3 ft) in length and has only one cutting edge. This weapon dates back to the Han period but it has been considerably modified since that time. It is a traditional weapon of both Shaolin and tai-chi and was used in the Boxer Rebellion and later during the war with Japan (1937-45).

The *san cha* (trident)

The *san cha* has a trident-shaped head and is mounted on a long pole in the same manner as other shaft-type weapons. The origin of the weapon is not clear; however, at Yun Kang in Shansi there is a fifth-century Buddhist figure carrying a similar type of trident weapon. The prongs of the fork are used for thrusting, ensnaring and blocking attacks. The *san cha*, a popular weapon in southern China, may originally have had agricultural connections.

The *san chet kwon* (three-sectioned staff)

The *san chet kwon* consists of three sections of wooden rod, 2.5-6 cm (1-1½ inches) in diameter, which are joined by chain links. The weapon can be swung to give over a 3 metre (9 ft) defensive radius or used in 1 metre (3 ft) sections to block, parry, thrust or strike. In one of the Shaolin style uses of this weapon, a most difficult manoeuvre is a spinning jump, while passing the *san chet kwon* under the legs, over the body and ending in an overhead block. For the novice, in the early days of training the centre pole will always catch under the feet on landing, forcing the two outer poles from the hands sending them smashing across either shin, while on landing the centre pole wedges painfully under the arches of the feet. Masters, however, are capable of jumping high into the air while applying this form.

The *cha* (truncheon)

The *cha* is a steel truncheon-like weapon with a tine (prong) either side of the handle pointing outwards. The origin of this weapon is hard to pinpoint. It is similar to the Okinawan weapon called a *sai*; in Fukien it is called the *titjio* and in Indonesia it is known as the *tjbang*. There were early links between China, India and Indonesia and mythological Indian deities, such as Siva, prince of demons, are depicted carrying a small hand trident which may have been the founding idea of this type of weapon. The introduction of iron came to Indonesia some time after that of China and India; however it is possible that this weapon developed independently there. The techniques of the *cha* include thrusting, striking, hitting and ensnaring the attacker's weapon in either tine. It is never used for cutting as it is not a bladed weapon. *Cha* are often used in pairs.

Deadly chopsticks

There are many lesser-known 'weapons' that have been developed from everyday items but are not common to the various styles of Chinese boxing. The use of chopsticks was not only confined to eating; some masters developed techniques with them for attacks on sudden encounter. The chopsticks could be flicked from their resting place on the table straight into the hands and used for striking and thrusting. Coins were sometimes thrown at an attacker to distract him while a substantial defensive move was made. One old master known to the author concealed sharp needles in his mouth. He could eat and drink with them in position, but when attacked he would blow them with great accuracy into the attacker's face. The old man was not even prepared to pass his skill on to his sons and because he found no one with whom to entrust the moral responsibility that went with such knowledge, it died with him.

The student's search

The spear, broadsword, staff, straight sword and halberd are among the main weapons utilized in modern-day Chinese boxing styles. The defensive tactics of the weapons often correspond to the four directions of the compass, giving all-round defensive and offensive ability. In many modern Chinese weapons skills the original fighting strategy has given way to the development of form and style, which makes them less practical in the original situations for which they were designed. However, there also exist the formal training methods of the old traditions which have retained the manner of tuition and the techniques passed down from earlier times.

Those who are looking for a school of Chinese boxing, whether it encompasses weapons or not, will need to set certain specific goals in their own mind before beginning the search. It is not hard to find a school that teaches the modern concepts, but the old traditions offer a greater challenge for the modern exponent. The first step is to find the school, the second is to be accepted, the third to endure the training, the fourth to retain the humility as the skill develops, and the fifth to bear the responsibility of the knowledge when you are skilled. This path represents a lifetime's study in a chosen skill, for there is a Chinese saying by Kang-hsi: 'If you reject iron, you will never make steel.'

Right: *The **san cha** is a trident popular in southern China. Its origins are shrouded in mystery but it may have been carried by some Buddhist priests in ancient times.*

Below: *The unique Chinese art of the rope is demonstrated by master Liu Huailiang, who is a national champion and **wu-shu** exponent.*

The classical warrior of Japan, called
bushi, represented both the heart of feudal
history and the martial tradition.

6

JAPAN'S MARTIAL TRADITIONS

T he samurai are at the core of Japan's martial tradition. However, the spirit that pervades their tales of valour is found deep-rooted in the legends and history of their nation. According to legend, after Izanagi formed the islands of Japan by withdrawing his lance from the sea, he and his sister descended to the islands. Izanami died giving birth to the fire god and Izanagi sought for her in the bowels of the earth, where the lord of the underworld guarded the immortal spirits of the dead. Like the Greek legend of Orpheus, who searched in the underworld to return his love Eurydice to life, Izanagi returned empty-handed.

While washing in the sea, Izanagi gave birth to various deities; his nose gave birth to the storm god Susanowo and as in the Chinese legends of P'an ku (see Chapter 3), his left eye became the sun goddess and his right eye the moon goddess. The sun goddess Amaterasu had an argument with the storm god and hid in a cave. As a result of this the world was plunged into darkness and the inhabitants of the islands devised a plot to induce her into the open. They danced before the entrance and as the goddess became curious they held a mirror before the entrance. She saw her reflection and, thinking she had been replaced, rushed from the cave. Immediately the entrance was sealed by a mystical rope to prevent her returning and in this way light was restored to the earth. To this day, the mirror and the sacred rope can be seen in Shinto shrines throughout Japan.

Beginnings of a new nation

Japan's earliest inhabitants, arriving perhaps by crude canoes, discovered the islands a mere 5,000 years ago. These people may have been ancestors of the Ainu, who are of Caucasian origin and who still speak their own language. There were undoubtedly other early settlers, from China, Korea and Mongolia. By 660 BC one of the latter-mentioned peoples arrived in Kyushu and drove back the original inhabitants, who may have been largely of Ainu stock, and established a religion based on earlier ethnic beliefs which eventually formed the Shinto religion of Japan.

Japan is first mentioned in a Chinese document from the third century AD Wei dynasty where it is referred to as 'Wa'. The document mentions a queen called Himiko who ruled from a province in Kyushu and the type of arms used in battle. These were the Japanese bow and bamboo arrows with iron or bone tips, iron shields, swords and halberds. There is no mention of horses so we must assume that the warriors of this period fought on foot. In fact there was evidence that during the earlier Han dynasty emissaries of both nations visited each other and cultural exchanges took place.

By the fifth century the capital had moved to Asuka and in 552 the king of Paikche in Korea sent an envoy to Japan with a bronze statue of Buddha, together with certain other religious scriptures. There were two opposing schools of thought concerning the new religion. One clan, called Mononobe and of Japanese descent, opposed Buddhism, but others, such as the Hata and Soga clans that were made up of naturalized Japanese, favoured the new religion. The outcome of the bloody encounters that ensued saw the Soga clan victorious. The first Japanese Buddhist temple was built in Asuka and Shotoku Taishi became crown prince. During this reign he established a social structure based on Confucianism, strengthened relationships with China and expounded the Buddhist scriptures.

Various expeditions established a firm cultural link with the T'ang dynasty in China and many Chinese traditions were established in Japan. After the death of Shotoku and the overthrow of the Soga rule, the Taika Reform (645-701), which established land tenure, taxes and the control of the clans under the emperor, came into force. Its edicts were based on the knowledge of the Chinese T'ang government. During this period most swords were either imported or made by Korean or Chinese smiths. They were straight bladed and inferior in quality to the later curved blades.

Dawn of the samurai

The Taika Reform marked the start of the Nara period and the establishment of the new capital at Nara, which was fashioned on the Chinese capital of Ch'ang during the Sui dynasty. Equally important, its inception changed the obligations of the nation. Ranks were established for officials, each with their respective benefits, and taxes became universal, much like the tithing systems of feudal England. Farmers were conscripted for certain periods, to serve either as imperial guards, border guards or as local militia. Buddhist priests, too, were expected to fight for the local lords when called upon to do so in the name of the emperor, or in order to protect their monasteries.

In 794 the capital was moved to Heian (modern-day Kyoto) and the samurai development began to take place. Conscripted farmers proved to be ineffective and untrained in battle so the emperor Kammu ordered the sons of noblemen to take their place. These men, called *kondei*, had experience in military skills, as did the monastery-trained warrior monks called *sohei*. Whilst the local landowners trained more warriors on their growing estates, and whilst the imperial court continued to study Chinese classics and Chinese writing gradually began to develop into a recognizable Japanese script, law and order began to break down. One clan called the Fujiwara grew in strength and through intermarriage gained political advantage until its power was greater than that of the emperor and a dictatorship was established.

Right: Pottery figures were placed round the tombs of the early Japanese emperors. These give us a good idea of what the forerunners of the samurai must have looked like.

Left: *Armies of warrior monks were a formidable presence throughout Japan in the eleventh and twelfth centuries. They wore armour under their clerical robes and carried, among other weapons, the* **naginata.**

Struggle of the clans

The tenth century marked a more independent Japan and breaks were made with both China and Korea. By 967 Fujiwara Saneyori was made regent and the first use of the word 'samurai' appeared, the word deriving from the verb 'sameru' which means 'to serve'. It described the warriors who acted as bodyguards to protect nobles and noted figures. This era also marked the birth of the true Japanese sword. A smith called Yasutsuna from the province of Hoki produced tempered steel blades with the familiar curved single cutting edge of the samurai sword. The halberd played an important role in battlefield strategy, as did the bow and arrow and the horse. Some sword blades were over 1.2 metres (4 ft) long. Armour developed a distinctive Japanese flavour and was worn particularly by the mounted warrior. It consisted of sections for the front, back, sides, collar, shoulders and legs. The whole suit was made up of small laced plates of either iron or thick leather which were then lacquered, the helmet being constructed in a similar manner.

By the early part of the eleventh century the Fujiwara regents had a strong allegiance with a clan called the Minamoto, while the ex-emperor Shirakawa favoured another clan called the Taira. The metropolitan police bureau (*Kebiishi-cho*) were unable to cope with the rise in robbery and other crimes. These problems

were compounded by the Buddhist monks who not only fought amongst themselves but waged frequent protests at the capital. These *sohei* had developed into powerful religious armies, protecting the monasteries. Among the most powerful groups was that of the Enryakuji temple, which on one occasion sent thousands of armour-clad *sohei* wielding awesome *naginata* (halberds) down to the capital to protest against the Onjoji temple having separate rights. After bitter arguments over a period of years a massive and bloody confrontation took place when the Enryakuji *sohei* besieged the Onjoji temple. In the battle, *naginata* flashed, limbs were severed and bodies lay everywhere. Thousands of *sohei* fought until the Onjoji temple with over 24,000 holy scriptures was razed to the ground.

By the middle of the twelfth century, a confusing state of affairs existed. It was not uncommon for an emperor to rule as a cloistered emperor while a titular emperor remained in power. At the same time, the Fujiwara clan controlled the military situation, with their strength gained from eliciting the help of either the Minamoto or Taira clans — who in turn obtained strength of numbers from the *sohei* of various monasteries. There was a great deal of confused warfare which culminated in the confrontation between the Minamoto and Taira clans.

The first insurrection, called Hogen, came in 1156 but the

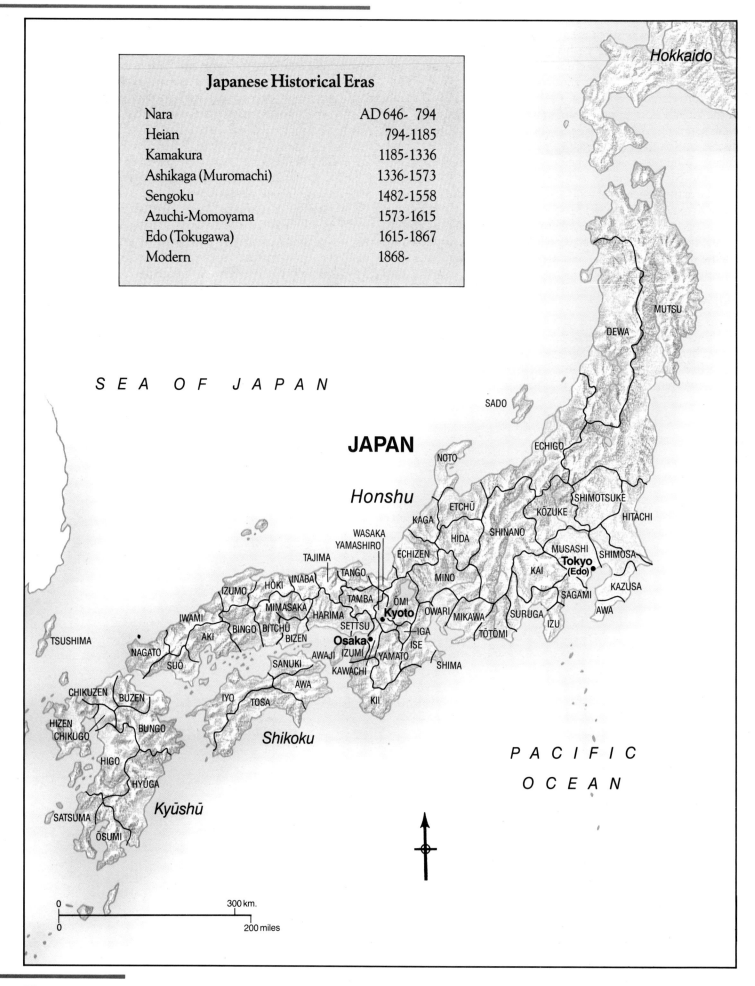

Japanese Historical Eras	
Nara	AD 646- 794
Heian	794-1185
Kamakura	1185-1336
Ashikaga (Muromachi)	1336-1573
Sengoku	1482-1558
Azuchi-Momoyama	1573-1615
Edo (Tokugawa)	1615-1867
Modern	1868-

Hokkaido

SEA OF JAPAN

JAPAN

Honshu

MUTSU

DEWA

SADO

ECHIGO

NOTO

SHIMOTSUKE

KAGA   ETCHŪ   KŌZUKE   HITACHI

HIDA   SHINANO

WASAKA
YAMASHIRO   ECHIZEN

TAJIMA   TANGO   MINO   MUSASHI   SHIMOSA

INABA   KAI   **Tokyo (Edo)**

IZUMO   HŌKI   TAMBA   ŌMI   OWARI   SAGAMI   KAZUSA

IWAMI   MIMASAKA   HARIMA   MIKAWA   SURUGA   AWA

AKI   BINGO   BITCHŪ   SETTSU   IGA   TŌTŌMI   IZU

TSUSHIMA   BIZEN   **Kyoto**

NAGATO   AWAJI   ISE

SUŌ   SANUKI   IZUMI   **Osaka**   YAMATO   SHIMA

CHIKUZEN   BUZEN   KAWACHI

IYO   AWA   KII

HIZEN   BUNGO   TOSA

CHIKUGO

HIGO   *Shikoku*

HYŪGA   *Kyūshū*

PACIFIC
OCEAN

SATSUMA

ŌSUMI

0 _____ 300 km.
0 _____ 200 miles

Minamoto clan was suppressed and its leader Tameyoshi was ordered to be decapitated by his son. He refused and the task went to another. The second uprising came when the leader of the Taira clan, Kiyomori, left the capital on a short journey. The Minamoto clan took advantage of this chance and took control of the Great Palace in the capital in what became known as the Heiji Uprising. When Kiyamori had returned to the Heian district of Rokuhara he started to plan the attack on the Great Palace. Whilst this was happening the emperor Nijo escaped from the palace disguised as a serving maid. For a while the defence of the palace went well for the Minamoto clan. However, when Kiyomori gave the impression that some of his troops were retreating, Minamoto troops followed in hot pursuit, leaving a gaping hole in their defences. The Taira clan then crushed the enemy with the help of the *sohei* from the Hiyeizan temple and sent them fleeing in defeat.

Fall of the Minamoto

It was a cold winter's night as the Minamoto leader Yoshitomo and three of his sons crossed the snow-covered mountains to obtain help from the east. The youngest son, only in his early teens, had been wounded in battle and slowed down the party, so at his own request Yoshitomo took his life rather than let the

enemy find him. Some short while after their escape Yoshitomo was himself slain by a traitor in his troops and Kiyomori had Yoshitomo's two sons Yoritomo and Yoshitsune sent into exile. Yoshihara, another of Yoshitomo's sons, was put to death. Taira no Kiyomori was supreme and the Taira clan governed Japan.

The two sons of Yoshitomo never forgot their family plight and bided their time as their age and strength grew. There is a folk tale about one of the sons, Yoshitsune. When he was a lad of twelve, it was said that he received secret tuition on the sword arts from *tengu* — mountain demons who were expert swordsmen and skilled in all the martial arts. One day he came to a bridge and encountered Benkei, who was a warrior priest from the Enryakuji temple. Benkei was no ordinary man. He possessed an explosive temper and was as strong as Samson. The priest had held the bridge against all who had wanted to cross, collecting their swords as a toll. Those who fought were defeated or fled in terror of the *naginata* he wielded. The young Yoshitsune refused to pay the toll and began to cross the bridge, while at the same time playing his flute. The enraged Benkei swung at him with his *naginata* but light as a feather Yoshitsune sprang clear and struck the *naginata* from Benkei's hands with his flute. The monk was so amazed at the courage and skill of this young boy that for ever after he became his henchman and servant.

Right: *The act of* **seppuku** *was committed with the utmost integrity, conforming to rigid custom and formality (see Chapter 7).*

The Gempei war

In 1180 the Minamoto reprisal started, headed by Yoritomo. Thus the struggle known as the Gempei war had begun. Kiyomori, fearing the opposition of the Kofukuji and Todaiji monasteries, ordered their destruction, which turned them against the Taira clan. On 21 March 1181 Kiyomori passed away from natural causes. The warring continued with the Minamoto troops being led by Yoshitsune and Yoritomo. Eventually, at the battle of Dannoura in 1185, the Minamoto clan were victorious and its leader Yoritomo set up his capital in Kamakura and established a military government *(bakufu)*, while the imperial court remained in Kyoto. Yoritomo, a frugal man who ruled with both wisdom and firmness, held the respect and allegiance of all his fighting men. It was at this time that a strict social structure began to evolve, with the warrior at the top of the social scale. The term bushi (knight) personified the warrior class rather than the term samurai (servant), but to become a bushi required the approval of shogun (military commander) Yoritomo and was the birthright of noble stock. A strong policing system was introduced and the warrior code of ethics known as Bushido developed, placing loyalty above life.

The code of Bushido established the concepts of *giri* and *gimu*, which were founded on obligation and gratitude. The lord housed, fed and looked after his samurai, who in return were prepared to give their lives for the lord as warriors and gentlemen. On certain occasions the samurai were expected to take their own lives. This act was called *seppuku* (in the vulgar tongue *harakiri*). If a samurai was faced with capture by the enemy, then he was expected to take his own life; conversely, if a samurai committed an offence which was punishable by death, then he was again expected to take his own life rather then be killed by the public executioner (see Chapter 7).

Yoshitsune, the brother of Yoritomo, lived in Kyoto but as time went on he became influenced by the soft life and the political desires of the imperial court. After an attempt on his life and accusations by his brother, he went into hiding with his family and faithful servant Benkei. There are many tales of Benkei's protection of his master. One story relates how Benkei, acting as a rearguard and wielding his *naginata* while Yoshitsune and his family escaped, left bodies waist high. Eventually, his own body was pierced with hundreds of enemy arrows and knowing that death was upon him, he secured his hands to his *naginata* and propped himself up so that the enemy would believe him to be still alive and therefore keep their distance. Yoshitsune was eventually

cornered and took his own and his family's life to prevent capture. His head was removed by the high constable Yasuhira and placed in *sake* to preserve it. It was then presented before Yoritomo as proof of the deed.

After Yoritomo's death at the age of 52, his sons ruled in succession as shogun. However, none of them had either the wisdom or the strength of their father. Thus began a confusing time during which the wife of Yoritomo and her father Tokimasa ruled as regents, governing the successive shogun, and for almost 100 years power was held by a succession of regents from the Hojo clan. In the course of time Yoritomo's sons were either assassinated or suffered premature death and so his family line ended. The emperors still functioned on the titular and cloistered principle, retaining only their temporal rights with little material power. The Buddhist monasteries, too, continued to harass the capital with unwarranted demands.

During this era the skills of swordmaking flourished and produced one of Japan's most noted masters of the trade, Masamune, whose swords can be seen today as sharp and as polished as the time they were crafted. Armour became more complex and some vulnerable areas at the side and shoulders were given greater protection, while the front section was

invariably made of iron or iron plates which were overlapped for strength. The swords hung at the side with the cutting edge down, which made drawing and cutting from horseback a great deal easier. The cavalry also used the Japanese bow which had the nocking point two-thirds of the way down, again allowing added manoeuvrability from horseback. On the battlefield the footsoldier used a long spear or halberd but wore little or no armour.

Opposite: Minamoto Yoshitsune (on horseback) leading his army against Sakurama Yoshitsura at the battle of Katsu-ura during the Gempei wars.

Below left: Swordsmith Sanjo Anjo Kokagi Murechika forging a blade in the grounds of Inauri temple.

*Below right: A warrior of the lower classes. He holds a **nagamaki** – a cross between a **naginata** and a long sword.*

Following pages: The famous meeting at the bridge between the young Minamoto Yoshitsune and the warrior-priest Benkei. From a woodcut by Kuniyoshi.

The divine wind

In 1260 Kublai Khan established Mongol rule in China and in an effort to extend his rule sent envoys to Japan with demands. However, Japan responded by having them executed. In response to this and after several small skirmishes on the southern island of Kyushu, in 1281 the main Mongol assault was launched with an army of over 400 ships and 100,000 men. For once Japan was united in repelling the intruders and great armies were sent to Kyushu, where the battle raged for several months. In the month of August a great typhoon came and wiped out almost all of Kublai Khan's men and ships. The battle was over, the 'divine wind' had changed the scales of fortune, and Kublai Khan never returned to Japan's shores.

In the ensuing years few emperors held any real power except one, Go-daigo, who came to the throne in 1318. By this time the country was once again in turmoil, with many samurai unhappy about the structure of the ruling powers. Go-daigo tried to remedy this situation with the introduction of Confucian principles from China, with himself in position at the top of the pyramid. He made several attempts to overthrow the military rule of Kamakura, helped by the brilliant general Kusunoki Masashige (see Chapter 2), but unfortunately Go-daigo was a bad judge of character and this was to be his downfall.

In 1333 Go-daigo defeated the Hojo regents, partly due to the strategy of Masashige and as a result of one general, Takauji of the Ashikaga clan, who changed sides. The last Hojo regent, together with more than 200 of his samurai, committed *seppuku* rather than be captured, thus ending the Hojo line.

Ashikaga Takauji was clever, cunning and ambitious. He gained the confidence of Go-daigo, while turning all others against the emperor by spreading exaggerated rumours. The samurai who had helped Go-daigo to power were the least rewarded and only staunch supporters like Masashige remained loyal to him. Takauji even turned the emperor against his own son prince Morinaga, who was banished and later assassinated. By the time Go-daigo realized his failings, Takauji had both the power and the armies to support him. Go-daigo's final error of judgement came when he went against Masashige's advice and ordered his armies to fight his arch-enemy general Takauji on his own ground in the south. This led to the destruction of his armies and the death of Masashige, as well as his own internment and death the following year.

Ashikaga power

General Takauji became shogun in 1338, establishing his capital in Kyoto. For a short while Japan saw two claims to the imperial throne, which was reconciled in 1392 when Go Komatsu became emperor. The Ashikaga period lasted for 200 years. Trade was established with China once again and taxes were forced sky-high to cover the huge extravagances of the rulers. For instance, the seventh shogun Yoshimitsu had a pavilion of pure gold leaf built in Kyoto and the eighth shogun erected one of silver.

Although the arts flourished, the government and court in the capital were so busy with their pleasures that law in the provinces began to break down and landowners recruited more and more samurai as they fought among themselves for greater power. During this era schools of martial training developed, where the warrior could study weapon skills, battle strategy, field

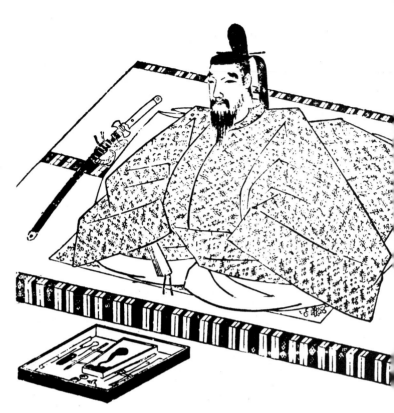

Above: *The emperor Go-daigo – with the help of Masashige – defeated the Hojo regents, but was himself deposed by the Ashikaga clan.*

period, called Tenshin Shoden Katori Shinto Ryu, is still in existence today. Its founder, Iizasa Choisai Ienao (1387-1488), was born in Chiba prefecture and came from a country samurai family. The weapons of the school included spear, halberd, sword, staff, jujutsu and many other skills. Zen Buddhism flourished among the samurai class, helping them to come to terms with the nature of both life and death.

The armour and battlefield tactics of the samurai underwent further modification during the Ashikaga era. Helmets became more elaborate, cheek and neck guards were added and chain mail was introduced for arm and leg protection. The skill called *kumi uchi* (armour grappling) developed, in which the samurai trained in techniques of thrusting a dagger through weak points in the armour and into vital organs. Empty-hand techniques were also employed, but these were very simple and robotic. Once the armour-clad warrior was thrown to the ground it was not easy for him to get up, especially considering that the armour weighed 36 kg (80 lbs) or more. Footsoldiers were playing a more permanent part in warfare but the spear and halberd were still favoured weapons.

In 1467 the whole country was thrown into a bloody civil war (the Onin war) which lasted ten years. From its conclusion until 1558 the land was in a state of anarchy, local warlords strengthening their domains and employing huge armies to govern and protect their lands and to wage war on neighbours in order to expand their territories. The fighting skills of the samurai developed tremendously throughout this period as they were never short of practice in both tactics and warfare.

Right: *Not only the* **bushi** *had face protection. Even footsoldiers wore plates to protect the brow and cheeks.*

Right below: *This style of helmet – known as* **tatami kabuto** *– gave extra protection for the neck.*

Below: *During the Ashikaga era armour improved, cheek and neck guards were introduced, as well as chain mail for protecting the limbs.*

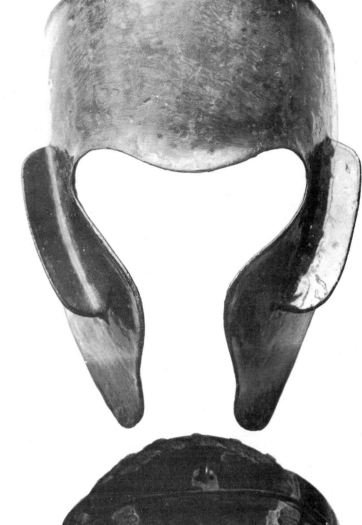

A horseman at the battle of the River Uji in 1184 fought between the armies of rival generals Sasaki Takatsuna and Kajiwara Kagesuye.

Left: *Osaka castle, the site of the decisive battle in 1614 in which Hideyori attempted to overthrow Ieyasu. The attempt failed and both Hideyori and his mother perished.*

From anarchy to unity

The sixteenth century rings with the tales of great samurai heroes, such as Takeda Shingen, born in Kai. When Shingen became lord of Kai, like the other lords of his time he fought to enlarge his domain. His arch enemy, Uesugi Kenshin, was lord of the Echigo and both men fought frequently to become the dominating power; in fact Kenshin's motto was 'power controls power'. On one occasion at the battle of Kawanakajima in 1559 Shingen sent 18,000 of his troops behind mount Saijo for a rear attack, which left him with some 2,000 men in the main camp. Kenshin anticipated this strategy and made a dawn attack with his army of 13,000 men. Shingen was taken by surprise but defended well while awaiting the return of his main army. Shingen was directing his troops from the centre of the camp, armed only with a *gumbaiuchiwa* (iron war fan). Suddenly out of the mist came Kenshin, riding a mighty horse and brandishing his *katana* (sword). He circled Shingen and cut at his head, but Shingen warded off the cut with the iron fan. Three more cuts were made and equally well deflected, except the last, which ripped the fan in two and drew blood from Shingen's forehead. As the final blade of death descended, fate intervened. A spear thrust bolted Kenshin's horse and spared Shingen.

In 1559 Oda Nobunaga became master of Owari. He was a rash man but a skilful samurai who began the task of unifying Japan. He was joined by warlords Hideyoshi and Ieyasu, who gave him their constant support. When Portuguese Jesuits began to arrive on the shores of Japan, Nobunaga encouraged trade with the West — perhaps his interest lay in their firearms which were introduced in 1582. He had no love for the Buddhists and in 1571 his troops totally destroyed their headquarters at Hiyeizan where monks, *sohei*, women and children were all slaughtered and the whole place razed to the ground.

Nobunaga's other main problem was Takeda Shingen, so he prepared for a final encounter with him. However, in the meantime Ieyasu's troops had been involved with Shingen in a small skirmish, where the latter had been wounded. Shingen died later from his wounds and his men tried to keep the fact secret without success. Shingen's next of kin Takeda Katsuyori fought Nobunaga in Echizen but his troops were easily defeated by Nobunaga's use of firearms. Nobunaga then pushed forward to overthrow Kenshin and established control of the Echizen province. Both Hideyoshi and Ieyasu continued to gain territory and were united in their efforts with Nobunaga, whose death due to an act of folly some time earlier was imminent. During a drinking bout Nobunaga had tapped one of his generals, Mitsuhide, on the head with his fan and made some jest. Mitsuhide had been deeply offended and harboured a grudge which he repaid by assassinating Nobunaga in 1582.

Hideyoshi quickly avenged Nobunaga's death and together with Ieyasu took control of the unification of Japan which was completed by 1590. Although the task of administration lay ahead, Buddhism and Christianity flourished, more foreigners came to Japan and a largely redundant army was employed by Hideyoshi to wage war on Korea. This invasion was not a success but showed Japan that their weakness lay in sea power.

During Hideyoshi's lifetime Ieyasu remained in Edo (modern-day Tokyo) and after his death in 1598 he at first took no part in the running of the country. But as things again began to fall apart he stepped in and in 1600 confronted the protagonists at the battle of Sekigahara, about 80 kilometres (50 miles) from Kyoto. After a decisive victory he became shogun and ruled from his capital in Edo, while the imperial court remained in Kyoto. In 1614 the young son of Hideyoshi, called Hideyori, gathered many samurai around him at Osaka castle in a bid to overthrow Ieyasu. But the castle fell, Hideyori and his mother died and the line of Hideyoshi ended.

Warfare over the previous decades had changed considerably, armour was made to withstand firepower and the musket took its place in the warrior's arsenal. The bow took a secondary place in battle, being mainly used to pick out key figures in combat. The sword and spear remained popular but the halberd declined.

Among the famous swordsmen of the period was Miyamoto Musashi (see Chapter 2). Another famous figure was a shipwrecked English sailor called Will Adams, a ship's pilot by trade. Ieyasu befriended him and sought his knowledge of shipbuilding. In Japan he became known as Mura Anjin, he took a Japanese wife and was buried in Yukoska near Yokohama. In recent years his life was portrayed in the novel *Shogun*.

The misguided loyalists

Throughout Ieyasu's lifetime foreign trade grew, but the Christians began to interfere in Japan's politics, presenting an increasing threat to his position. With Ieyasu's death in 1616 his son Hidetada became shogun and the persecution of Christians grew to epidemic proportions, culminating in the seclusion policy which banned any kind of foreign contact. During the period of seclusion, which lasted until 1853, the feudal system flourished and a strict class system was established with the samurai at the top of the tree, followed by the farmers, then the artisans and merchants. Taxes were heavy and often a lord would forfeit his land, leaving his samurai unemployed. During this period the number of masterless samurai (*ronin*) grew to over 300,000 and one misguided loyalist, called Yui Shosetsu, saw how these *ronin* could be united as an army against the shogun.

Yui Shosetsu was born in 1605 and at the age of 16 went to Edo, where he met a descendant of Masashige, called Kusunoki Buden, who taught him everything about military science and the samurai skills. Shosetsu established an academy for the *ronin* and, uniting them to his cause, by 1651 he was ready to effect his plan. Unfortunately for him some government spies had infiltrated his movement and related the plot to the shogun, so a warrant was issued for his arrest. At first he avoided capture but he was finally cornered at an inn. Over 100 armed police surrounded the inn but Yui Shosetsu and eight of his co-conspirators committed *seppuku* rather than face capture. Soon after another 40 were arrested and put to death.

The family of Ieyasu were of Tokugawa stock and after his death successive members off the family ruled as shogun. During the rule of the fifth Tokugawa shogun, Tsunayoshi, an event occurred that reflected the ethics of Bushido and the loyalty of the samurai. The lord of Ako castle, Naganori Asano, had been tricked into looking foolish at the shogun's castle in Edo, by a superior called Yoshinaka Kira who was the overseer of ceremonies. Because deep disgrace was caused Lord Asano demanded an apology but Lord Kira simply mocked him. Unable to stand any more Lord Asano drew his dagger and cut Lord Kira across the face. The drawing of any blade within the precincts of the palace was an offence punishable by death and Lord Asano was sentenced to death by *seppuku*.

After the sentence had been carried out Asano's estate was forfeited and his retainers became *ronin*. However, it was generally felt that Lord Kira was to blame, so the *ronin* decided to avenge the death of their lord, who had been a fair and just man. The senior retainer, Yoshitaka Oishi Kuranosuke, signed a pledge in blood with 47 of the loyal retainers of Lord Asano to avenge his death, but because government spies were watching for just such an event they each pretended to go their separate ways. At last the stage was set when the government relaxed its vigilance and dropped their guard on Lord Kira. On 14 December 1702 the 47 retainers of Asano, led by Kuranosuke, raided his mansion under cover of a snowstorm. Many of Kira's men were killed but Kira himself was not to be found. A search revealed him in a cupboard in the women's quarters. He was given the chance to take his own life; he refused, so the retainers beheaded him.

The head was taken to their lord's grave and washed in a well, then presented before the tomb of their late master. All the retainers gave themselves up to the justice of the time and each was sentenced to death by *seppuku*. On 4 February of the following year sentence was carried out and they were buried beside their master. This act of total loyalty had such impact that even today on the anniversary of their deaths, thousands of Japanese go to the site of the graves at the Sengakuji temple and burn incense for the repose of the samurai's spirits.

Left: *In the precincts of the Sengakuji temple, the graves of the 47* **ronin** *– the loyal retainers of Lord Asano – remain to this day a testimony to their brave deed.*

Right: *This portrait of Oboshi Yuranosuke Yoshio depicts the noble face of loyalty and honour that made the deeds of the 47* **ronin** *possible.*

Left: *The Satsuma rebellion of 1877 constituted the last struggle of the samurai as a class. The rebellion left them defeated in battle but victorious in demonstrating the remarkable spirit and honour of the samurai.*

Right: *A group of Saigo Takamori's students preparing their strategy on the eve of the Satsuma rebellion.*

The samurai politician

Japan remained in a cocoon of feudal isolation, while the rest of the world forged forward into a modern industrial era. It was not until 1853 that she was awakened from her feudal slumber when Commodore Perry brought his fleet from America. Very soon Russia and Britain had also secured treaties and various legations were set up. However, Japan was aware of the manner in which China had been treated and showed considerable reserve. Hatred towards foreigners grew and there were many incidents where *ronin* assassinated the 'barbarians' (foreigners). Despite these incidents many Japanese went abroad to further their knowledge of the Western world.

One samurai who accommodated the changing times was Katsu Kaishu, born in Edo in 1823, the son of a lower-class samurai. Katsu Kaishu's family was very poor; however, he studied Zen and the way of the sword under his teacher Shimada Toranosuke. He trained hard to strengthen his spirit and after a day's training would go to the Oji shrine from his home in Akasaka, where he would perform a thousand cuts, meditate, then continue until dawn. Once he had attained inner enlightenment through his training he applied those principles to his everyday life. One example of this was in his effort to gain Western knowledge. He needed a good command of the Dutch language, but unable to afford the cost of a dictionary Katsu Kaishu hired one, made two complete copies, sold one to pay for

the hire fees, and kept the other for himself.

Katsu Kaishu travelled to both America and Britain, studying modern arms and naval matters. While he was away, hate grew against the shogun and foreigners in Japan. Assassins and extremists called *shishi* supported the emperor but opposed the shogun. On his return he established the beginnings of the modern Japanese nation. One day he was visited by Saigo Takamori, one of the heads of the Satsuma clan from Kyushu who were renowned warriors. They found themselves in agreement about the political situation and became good friends. In 1864 Kaishu, at the request of the shogunate, obtained the help of the Satsuma clan to suppress anti-government resurgence by the Choshu clan. In 1866 the 14th shogun died and the 15th shogun requested Kaishu to make peace with the Choshu clan, but his attempt was unsuccessful. The shogun then went behind Kaishu's back and in the war that followed in May 1867 the shogunate was defeated. In October 1867 the 15th shogun retired and returned the power of government to the emperor Meiji. In July 1868 the emperor Meiji left Kyoto for his new capital Edo, renamed Tokyo. Katsu Kaishu became vice-minister of the Japanese Navy. He once again took up residence in Akasaka and later became Japan's first Naval Minister. In 1875 Katsu Kaishu resigned his position, much to the disappointment of the government, as he was considered a Solomon among politicians.

His friend Saigo Takamori was at loggerheads with some

Left: *A statue of the great Saigo Takamori in Ueno park, Tokyo. With him is his dog and constant companion who died with his master on the battlefield.*

Right: *A Japanese diplomat resplendent in his samurai armour. Even into the modern era, the spirit of the medieval warriors remained at the heart of the Japanese nation.*

factions of the new government over the issue of Korea and when they refused to send a military expedition there, he resigned. Once back in Kyushu he established military schools for samurai, and began to form his own private army. In 1877 he led 40,000 samurai in the Satsuma rebellion. His army of Satsuma warriors, armed with traditional weapons, fought modern conscript troops using up-to-date firepower. After months of fighting and the deaths of over three-quarters of the samurai army, final defeat came for Takamori. He performed *seppuku* on the battlefield, laying beside the body of his dog that had been his constant companion through life. Some years later, at the instigation of Katsu Kaishu, the reputation of Saigo Takamori was re-established. His son was given a public position by the emperor and a statue was erected in his honour for his previous services to the emperor. In January 1899 Katsu Kaishu died at the age of 77.

Decline of the samurai

At the time of the Meiji Restoration there were over one million samurai in Japan. Although eventually many of them settled down to the new way of life, legislation governing their conduct was instituted. The wearing of swords was banned, feudal lords were deprived of their titles — although some became senior officials in the government — the position of samurai as a class was ended and all citizens were to be considered equal. Perhaps the final degradation for the samurai was the ordering of the removal of their traditional top-knot of hair, this loss of status hurting more than any other. After the Satsuma rebellion, the last samurai stand, Japan's long and bloody internal strife came to an end and society took up many of the ways of the West. However, beneath the peaceful surface the spirit and traditions of feudal Japan remained.

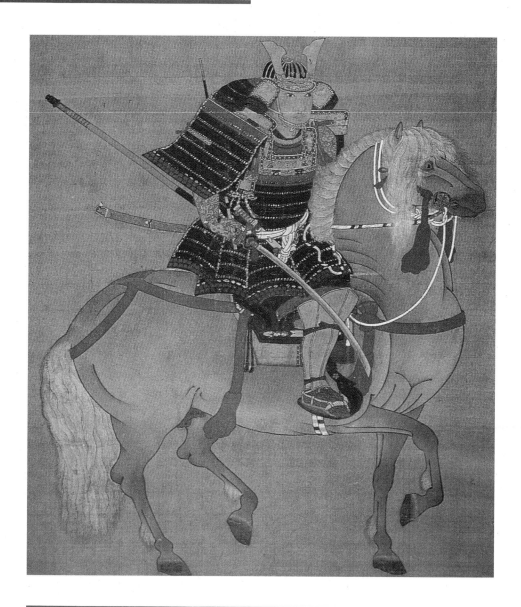

*The samurai spirit is a timeless heritage, born of an
age of war and bloodshed.*

7

THE SOUL OF
THE SAMURAI

T he samurai has perhaps the most compelling charisma of all the world's
fighting men. Yet to achieve any real understanding of the samurai class one
has to balance the ideal against the fallibility of human nature. He had the
reputation of being a man of emotionless stature, which constituted a mask that hid a
fearless warrior, his compassion tempered by the logic of reason of the rigid society in
which he lived. The reality, of course, rarely matched the myth. Some samurai were
cruel beyond measure, others wise or compassionate, some were greedy and licentious
and many more were none too skilful in the martial arts, hence they often lived short
lives.

The samurai status

In the Nara period (646-794) the name *kondei* was given to brave warriors, the sons of
noble families who were skilled in military arts. Later in the Heian period (794-1191) the
term 'samurai', the warriors who 'served' as retainers for the noted gentry, came into use.
By the time of the military ruler Yoritomo in the Kamakura period (1185-1335), a
warrior was called a *bushi*, which was a title equivalent to a knight in medieval Europe
and commanded the same status and respect.

There were many ranks of samurai covering a wide range of social status, which
changed from era to era. In the Edo period the shogun was the supreme military ruler,
the first major status group below him being the *daimyo*, who were lords of the manor
who owned estates and governed their own territories. Relatives of the *daimyo* were
called *kashin* and were given land in their families' domain and acted as family retainers.
The next group in the social scale of the samurai were the *hatamoto* who owned estates
and acted as commanders in the battlefield. There was also a lower status of *hatamoto*
called *go-kenin*, a term which dated back to the Kamakura period and referred to direct
vassals of the shogun.

The samurai represented the section of society that had the right to bear arms and
their status was dictated by their payment from their *daimyo*. In some cases this payment
would include land, but often the lower classes of samurai only received rice. The upper
classes of samurai entered battle on horseback; the lower classes attacked on foot, these
footsoldiers being called *ashigaru*. They wore light armour and carried only one main
weapon. The *ashigaru* constituted the lowest form of samurai rank. Below them were
assistants, such as the *chugen* and *zoshiki*, who were not allowed to carry swords.

A samurai of high rank was always attended when he went out. However, at night he
was always accompanied by a young samurai, a junior retainer called a *wakato* or

wakamusha, who was allowed to wear a sword and could therefore protect his master, as opposed to the *chugen* who were merely helpers. In the country areas many samurai families were also gentry from farming estates; these rural nobles were referred to as *ji* samurai. The *ronin* too were samurai that for some reason or another had no master to serve, for example if their lord had died in battle or his estate had been confiscated because of debt. These samurai were free to seek employment where they could. During the Tokugawa rule, however, they were often oppressed and sometimes even took employment as farmworkers.

During the comparative peace of the Tokugawa era many skilful swordsmen indulged in personal combat and challenges were commonplace. For example, if two samurai were walking in a crowded street and their scabbards knocked together, this was considered the equivalent to throwing down the gauntlet. If an apology was not instant, sword blades would flash until honour was satisfied. The young tearaways of that era used to wear their swords so that the scabbard stuck well out at the back in order to provoke a fight. The skilful samurai, however, would tuck his scabbard down so that he did not waste time being constantly challenged. However, crime increased and there were a great many street brawls; even the *chugen* formed gangs and robbed innocent city dwellers.

The samurai and civil law

Since the ninth century the warrior class had been responsible for maintaining the civil peace of the country, and thus one of the important roles that the samurai played in Japan's administration was that of the police force. The original police of that time were called *kebiishi,* but by the twelfth century the appointment had been taken over by *shugo* (constables) and *jito* (land stewards) who were appointed by the shogun from his most loyal warriors. These warriors had wide powers to enforce the law of the land. In fact many of the *shugo* later became *daimyo* (land barons) and administered their domains quite independently of the central government.

By the sixteenth century and the Tokugawa rule, various administrative powers controlled different aspects of government. The shogun selected his senior officials from *daimyo* and *hatamoto,* with a council of elders called *roju* who were directly responsible to the shogun. Below them were the *machi bugyo* (city commissioners) who exercised judicial and executive authority. There was one *machi bugyo* for Osaka, one for Kyoto, who also guarded the emperor's court, and two for Edo, one of whom acted in rota with the other as judge in serious crime cases. Under the *machi bugyo* were 25 senior police officers called *yoriki,* who were selected from samurai families. The *yoriki* were permitted to carry swords and to ride horses, wore a special style of kimono which reflected their rank, and had the power to act as judges in simple cases. They employed one hundred police officers called *doshin* for each of the two districts of Edo. These *doshin* were of low samurai rank and were only allowed to carry a short sword (*wakizashi*), iron truncheon (*jutte*) and a length of rope for restraining criminals.

The profession of police officer was hereditary for both the *yoriki* and *doshin.* Both received a salary from the government and were given extra rations to employ both official and unofficial helpers. The official helpers were called *komono* and were recruited from the common classes of Japan. Menial tasks were left to the unofficial helpers, *okappiki* and *meakashi,* and some of these assistants were ninja employed for undercover work.

Below and opposite: For the samurai, the wearing of their armour was both a complicated and skillful task. It had to be put on quickly and correctly with a strict method and order adhered to.

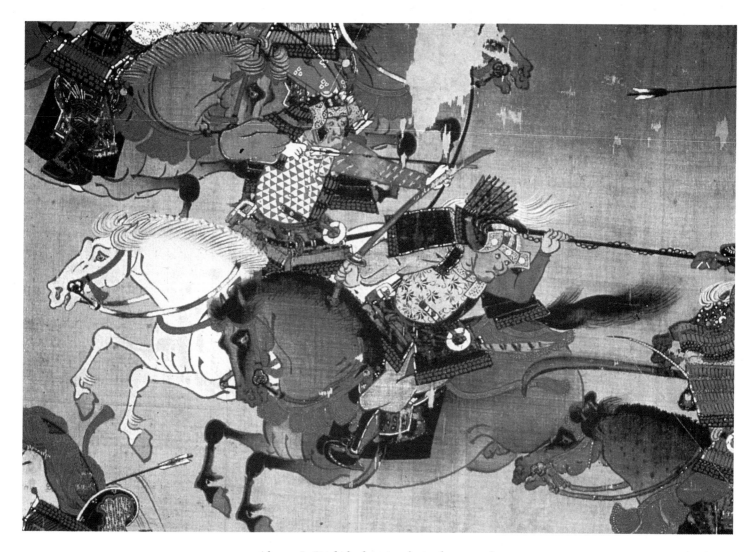

Above: In Bushido there is a fusion between the acceptance of death and the strength of life. When the **bushi** rode into battle he was prepared to die with dignity.

Right: Ieyasu, who died in 1598, was the last of the three great generals to complete the unification of Japan.

Enforcing the law

The only weapons that the common police could use for defence were *jutte* and rope, hence schools of restraining called hojojutsu and truncheon techniques called jutte jutsu developed within the police service. In the Edo period there existed over 200 styles of jutte jutsu used by the police. If an obstreperous person was using a sword, the *komono* had to arrest him by catching his blade in a small tine that protruded from the *jutte*, disarm him, then restrain the offender. Such techniques took uncommon courage and skill and many of the officers became expert in the use of *jutte*: any lack of skill meant premature death. Even after the national police force was founded in 1874, many still carried *jutte* unofficially.

Hemp rope was used to tie up prisoners and there were many methods of tying, depending on the social status of the prisoner and the crime that had been committed. Often the criminal would be knocked unconscious or restrained with a lock while he was being tied. Some of the techniques were very complex, allowing different limbs to be freed for eating or walking and then secured again. When carrying the rope it was tied in a special way and kept at the waist for easy access, then when it was required a man could be secured in under a minute. It was probable, however, that the lower-rank officers learned by experience rather than by organized martial arts study.

The law during the Tokugawa era (1615-1886) was harsh. Confessions were often obtained by torture, but only with the *roju's* consent. One method was to tie the victim and make him kneel on a deeply ridged board. Weights were then placed across his knees, causing the ridges to cut deeper into his shins until he confessed. Sentences for serious crimes varied: parent killers were crucified, arsonists were burned or decapitated, and robbers received very severe beatings. Some judges, however, had the wisdom of Solomon and minor offenders were usually fined.

If a swordsman was very skilful or tried to get past one of the many frontier posts set up throughout Japan, special techniques were employed. Men carrying *sodegarami*, consisting of a long hardwood pole encrusted with barbs along its first few feet, would be used to ensnare the kimono and twist up the cloth, thus restricting the attacker's movement. A *sasumata* was then used, which was a long pole with a double-tined fork at its very end. This was used to trap the neck and push the legs apart so that the attacker fell helpless and uninjured to the ground. Once disarmed he was taken away to face Tokugawan justice.

Bushido — the code of chivalry

Apart from the laws of the land, which the samurai administered at the direction of the shogun, he was bound by his own code of ethics called Bushido. This term has always been misunderstood by Westerners who often associate it with World War II and the actions of men who knew nothing of samurai history or philosophy. Bushido to the samurai was akin to the code of chivalry of the European knight. It encompassed his loyalty, courage, compassion, duty, humility, honour, faith, wisdom, obedience, justice, perseverance, frugality, sincerity and truth.

There is no exact written formula for the code of Bushido, but many of its examples and precepts have been recorded throughout Japan's history. It is clear from the chronicles of the Kamakura period, such as the *Tales of Hogen*, that the relationship between the samurai and his lord was very special, founded on duty and obligation, which the Japanese call *gimu*

Above: *Kaminoda and Draeger* **sensei** *demonstrating the use of the* **jutte,** *the traditional Japanese police weapon of restraint.*

and *giri*. This duty is tempered with Confucian thinking and goes hand in hand with gratitude, which even today plays an important role in Japan's society. In includes the duty to care for our parents who brought us into the world and made sacrifices to bring us up; this debt of gratitude is repaid by caring for them in later life. There is the duty to a friend who helps you in a time of great trouble; at that time you incur a lifelong unwritten obligation to return that favour when the need arises. Ignoring such obligations is like allowing dust to fall on the mirror of your true nature: one day you will peer into the looking glass and that nature will be obscured from view.

Duty and obligation to the lord were the cornerstones of the samurai existence. The contract between the two was only economic in so far as the lord would house and clothe the samurai. In return he would receive complete loyalty. Because the samurai was a warrior the loyalty went beyond his attachment to life itself — and even this was owned by the lord. To shun the obligations of death in the face of the enemy was the ultimate disgrace. To die without purpose, however, was not the way of the warrior. An example of this principle was when a samurai ran from a band of robbers who suddenly attacked him. Later when questioned about the incident he replied: 'My life is not mine to risk over personal matters; it belongs to my lord for whom I would willingly die.'

No man wishes to die — not even the samurai. But in facing the enemy, death was always a possibility and thus warriors sought to prepare themselves for that moment by turning to Zen Buddhism. As the cherry blossoms fade in their most beautiful

Above: *The understanding of* **gimu** *and* **giri** *(duty and obligation) was the cornerstone of the samurai's existence.*

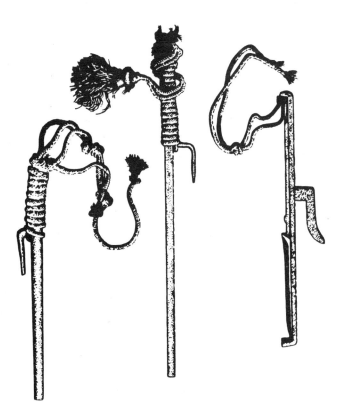

Below: **Jutte** *dating from the sixteenth and seventeenth centuries. Weapons such as these symbolized Japan's feudal police force.*

hour — they come and go before the end of spring yet how beautiful they look laying a pink mantle upon the ground — so the moment of death was both purposeful and beautiful for the samurai. One warrior, called Shigenari Kimura, would not let a morsel past his lips the day before a battle. He was prepared to die with dignity and did not want to secrete filth at the time of his likely death.

For the samurai the total acceptance of death came with non-attachment to life; each moment was enjoyed as if it were the last. This idea is well illustrated by the traditional story of a rich merchant who, although he had everything in life, still wanted to attain enlightenment through Zen. So he went to live in a monastery. After a few weeks he was no nearer to his quest and the head monk told him that it might take many years. 'I don't intend to waste all that time,' he exclaimed. 'Is there no short cut?' The head monk thought for a while, and then said, 'you are expert at chess. We have a young monk who is also expert; let's set up a game.'

The two men began to play and after an hour both were still equal. The rich merchant was relaxed and casual as he played; by contrast the young monk was attentive to the game. So the head monk called for his sword and explained to them that he intended to decapitate the loser. His expression convinced both players that he was serious. The rich merchant immediately began to concentrate. Sweat soaked his clothing and with each move he held his breath. A beam of sunlight shone across the floor, looking more beautiful than any he had ever seen before. All of a sudden he saw that the young monk had made a mistake. He glanced up

Left: *Many of Japanese film director Akira Kurosawa's classical masterpieces capture the frugal and strong spirit of the feudal warrior clans.*

Right: *One of the famous 47 **ronin** who went to their deaths to revenge the honour of their lord. The 47 **ronin** displayed a perfect attitude in the execution of their plot and the manner in which they submitted to the justice of the day.*

at his opponent's face; he too was trying to come to terms with the prospect of death. In an act of compassion the merchant overlooked his chance, but before he could make his move, with one sweep of his sword the head monk sent the chess board crashing to the floor. He then told the merchant that everything must be done as if it were a matter of life and death — even the playing of a game of chess.

In Bushido there is a fusion between the acceptance of death and the strength of life, which is reflected in the following tale. A farmer offended a *ronin* by accident and although he apologised, the *ronin* challenged him to a sword fight the following week. The farmer went to a famous teacher of swordsmanship that he knew and told him of his predicament. 'In so short a time no matter what I teach, you will certainly die next week, so you must get used to the idea', the farmer was told. The sword master then explained that although he must die, there was a chance that the farmer could also kill this offending *ronin*. 'No matter how you are attacked I will teach you one stance and one cut. Your opponent will first try you out but do not move. Only when he makes his cut will you make yours.' Knowing he was going to die, the farmer spent the week practising this one stance and cut.

When the time of the encounter came both men drew their swords, the farmer taking up his stance with his sword raised above his head. The *ronin* circled him and made some threatening gestures, but the farmer stood firm and faced his opponent. Knowing he would die he was totally committed to

delivering his one cut. Understanding the situation, the *ronin* lowered his sword and stood back. Then he spoke. 'When I challenged you I thought you were a country bumpkin, but I see that there is no opening in your defence without you rendering me a fatal cut and that you are totally committed to death. Such men are rare. The affair is over.'

In the seventeenth-century chronicles called the *Koyo Gunkan* there are many stories about the attitude expected of a samurai of any rank. Even among generals humility was considered an important attribute. If a general became conceited his appearance would naturally become undignified. There was great danger attached to being either too cowardly, too stupid — or even too strong. The ideal samurai faced victory and success without his character changing in any way and also faced defeat with dignity and suffering with indifference. In the words of Rudyard Kipling, the samurai could 'meet with triumph and disaster and treat those two imposters just the same'.

One of the most popular works on Bushido is called *Hagakure*. Written in the early eighteenth century by Yamamoto Tsunetomo for the Saga clan of Kyushu, in the opinion of the author it does not reflect the fundamental faith in humanity found in many of the earlier documents on the subject. Bushido is about duty and death, but more than that it sets the samurai the task of finding truth, polishing the mind and body and tempering the spirit through austere training. Bushido was the meeting place between the laws of nature and the philosophies of men.

Left: It is said in Japan even today that the spirit of the warrior remains with his armour. No one will ever wear the armour of another lest he inherits a weak spirit.

Right: Sentence of death or loss of face meant the act of **seppuku** for the samurai. This taking of one's own life was a solemn occasion – both the courage to live and the courage to die both being considered of great importance.

The samurai right to die by his own hand

The act of *seppuku*, which is commonly called *harakiri* (belly cutting), was only permitted for the samurai class. The warrior was allowed to take his own life to prevent loss of face, or when the sentence of death had been passed for a crime he had committed. In the latter case sentence was carried out formally, usually in the precincts of the local lord's palace. If the samurai was of high rank then the ceremony would be conducted indoors, but lower ranks were confined to the gardens of the household.

Many officials were present during the sentence, but the most important were the senior official, the prisoner, and the *kaishaku*, who were usually three samurai who ensured that the prisoner did not panic or try to escape. If he did so, then it was their job to kill him and remove his head. The senior *kaishaku* held a drawn sword out of sight of the prisoner who, as he disembowelled himself, would be decapitated. The head was then presented to the senior official for identification, thus completing the final act of the sentence.

Preparing for *seppuku* the prisoner would dress in his formal kimono, then be taken to the place of execution. He would sit on a raised mat facing west and a dagger would be brought to him on a wooden stand. In cases where it was thought he might use it to escape, only a fan or wooden dagger was brought. The *kaishaku* would then take his place facing north and a little out of the victim's view. The prisoner would slip the kimono from his shoulders and sit on the sleeves so that he would not fall backwards as he died. There was often a prearranged signal between the prisoner and principal *kaishaku*, who would take off the head before signs of pain brought disgrace on the prisoner.

The principal *kaishaku* had a difficult job and needed to be exceptionally skilled. Timing was of the utmost importance as the head had to be taken off before too much pain was experienced. The cut had to leave a little flesh attached to the neck so that the head fell face down into the lap, which prevented the indignity of revealing the prisoner's last expression. The remaining flesh was then cut and the head presented. Unfortunately, many *kaishaku* lacked the required timing and speed. Pain caused the shoulders of the condemned man to hunch and the sword would often go into the shoulder and not the neck, thus making several cuts necessary. This, apparently, was the fate experienced by Yukio Mishima, the well-known Japanese author, who committed *seppuku* on 25 November 1970.

When a samurai had to take his own life to prevent loss of face, the incident was often far from formal and often enacted in far from ideal conditions. The method used was again by disembowelment, but by cutting open the stomach death would not necessarily be instantaneous. So after the dagger or sword had been drawn across the stomach, it was inserted into the neck and pulled forward, almost certainly guaranteeing death. The women of a samurai family often carried a small dagger in the folds of their kimono and if their honour was violated they would plunge it into their heart or cut their throat. With such extreme ways of suicide, death was never taken lightly and only as a last resort.

Above: *The samurai was more than just a fearsome warrior dressed in armour. He was the sum total of all the heroic deeds of great samurai from a bygone era.*

Right: *A master swordsmith, dressed in a white robe and* **eboshi** *(black-lacquered hat), prepares to forge a samurai blade.*

The forging of a legend

The sword of the samurai was as much a reflection of his spirit as was the code of Bushido. The blade of pure tempered steel was imbued with the intrinsic soul of the smith who made it. It was a work of art, an instrument of death — and even a weapon that spared life. The blade was forged with religious ceremony and the smith purified himself before commencing the task.

The blade was forged from pure iron, the centre usually consisting of soft iron while the outside was hardened steel. This combination created a flexible blade with a hard outer surface for cutting and blocking. The smith beat and folded the metal many hundreds of times as he forged the blade, until it had stretched to its full length. The next step was to create the shape of the blade by cutting and filing; then the blade was tempered. The smith coated the blade in clay, leaving less where the tempering was required most. The blade was then heated in the forge and quickly plunged in a tank of water to be quenched.

The process of tempering was perhaps the most closely-guarded secret of the smith. The forge was kept in darkness so that the exact colour of the molten steel could be determined.

Even the temperature of the water into which it was plunged remained a mystery. Once in the feudal period an apprentice smith put his hand in the water to gauge its temperature. In an instant the smith had reached for a sword and had severed the offending hand from the wrist. The apprentice considered this loss was a fair price to pay for the knowledge of the temperature of the water and later became a master smith himself.

The blade was polished to a mirror finish to bring out the temper line and grain of the metal. Then the ornaments and scabbard were made with the same care and perfection. Many of the swords were given names and regarded with the same awe as Excalibur, the sacred sword of King Arthur. Early Japanese swords (up to about the year 900) were straight and were not forged in the traditional manner; they were called *ken* or *tsurugi*. The curved-blade sword, called a *tachi*, came into fashion with the development of cavalry, especially during the Heian period, and hung from the belt by two tapes, with the cutting edge facing downwards. Towards the end of the late Kamakura period swordmaking reached its zenith and the samurai began to wear the sword tucked in the belt with the cutting edge uppermost, this

Above and right: A samurai was never far from his
weapons – especially his sword. When his sword was
handed to another person, the cutting edge was
turned towards the giver, then turned towards the
receiver as he took hold of it.

sword being known as a *katana*. From the Ashikaga era it became fashionable for the samurai to wear both a long and short sword tucked through his belt. These matching swords were called *daisho*.

Sword ornaments often reflected the sword's purpose. Court and ceremonial types often displayed ostentatious sword furniture of gold and silver, while the working sword had a plain iron guard and fittings. A samurai was never far from his sword and many customs grew out of caution. If scabbards clashed it was a serious insult; likewise if a samurai was seated with his sword on the floor by his side and someone stepped over it there could be no forgiveness. When the warrior entered a house the sword was taken by a servant and kept by the door. However, the samurai still retained his short dagger in case of treachery. When the samurai was greeted by his host he would perform a kneeling bow. His left hand would go to the ground first as did the host's. After this the right sword hand of both would slide to the floor. As they rose it was the right sword hand that came to the knee first, followed by the left. If a sword was ever handed to another person, the cutting edge was turned towards the giver, then turned towards the receiver as he took hold of it. When death was an edge of pure cold steel caution and custom became one.

The samurai essence

The soul of the samurai was both intrinsic and real. It was in part his sword, his code of Bushido, his rigid custom, his inherent martial skills, and his deep insight of beauty. It was all these things — and yet much more. There was no one finger that you could point and say 'there goes a samurai'. He was more than just a fearsome warrior dressed in armour. He was an ideal, a spectre that was, and still is, both awesome and respected: the sum total of all the heroic deeds of great samurai from a bygone era.

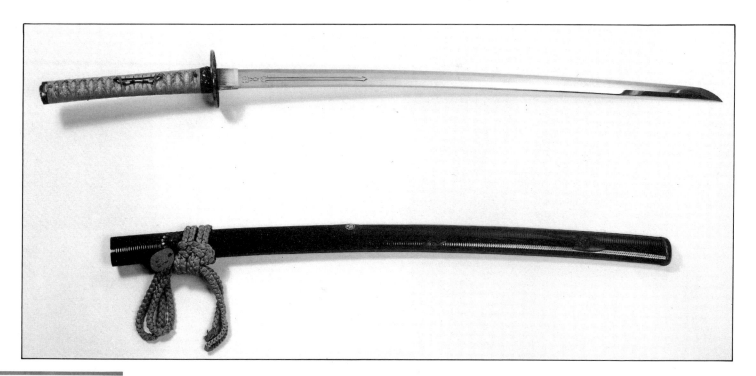

Blades of the master smiths. Above left: (left to right): **horimono** engraving by Sadakazu of Osaka; Tomomitsu of Bizen; Muramasa of Ise; Yasutsuna of Hoki.

Below left: A fine example of a seventeenth-century **katana** and its scabbard.

Above: Three sword blades in **tachi** mountings.

Below: An ornamented **tanto,** a short blade traditionally carried with the longer sword.

*From the skill of **bajutsu** (horsemanship) to the
extensive range of weapons in the warrior arsenal,
the samurai excelled in their search for perfection.*

8

THE WARRIOR ARSENAL

To understand the samurai skills it is important to know something of the structure of the *ryu* system. In ancient Greece those who sought to develop the intellect studied with great philosophers like Aristotle and Plato, who had founded a place of learning near Athens called the academy. It was neither a school nor a university, but a meeting place where philosophical and academic studies were passed on by the master. This institution constituted more of a family than a gathering of individuals. The Japanese warrior looked for his martial training in much the same way, by seeking formal tuition in what was called a *ryu*. The *ryu* was an academy of collective martial studies, but more than that it was a family founded by a great master skilled in fighting techniques whose reputation was highly regarded.

The ryu — a place of martial study

The *ryu* became the source of martial study in Japan as early as the fifteenth century with the founding of Katori Shinto Ryu near Sawara city. But there were undoubtedly *ryu* before that period which have not been so well documented. A noted samurai skilled in martial arts, with an undefeated reputation, would establish a *ryu*. Within the curriculum of the *ryu* there was a core weapon, usually the sword, around which the warrior was taught other weapons that he might encounter. In this way he had a working knowledge of the arms that his enemy could use and a knowledge of their limitations. All types of battle strategy and espionage were also part of the syllabus of many *ryu*.

The head master of the *ryu* sometimes had the support of a patron, usually a *daimyo* or higher-ranking person. Often a clan would employ a famous master who would teach all the warriors his *ryu*. The *ryu* was not something a samurai could just enter; in fact the existence of most *ryu* were kept a closely-guarded secret. If after various tests of integrity a samurai was admitted to a *ryu*, then in his own blood he had to sign a pledge not to reveal its secrets. To this day Katori Shinto Ryu keep up this practice.

To protect the existence of the *ryu* there was a strict structure of tuition. It was not uncommon for another master to send someone in to find a weakness in the style. Having learned what it was he would then challenge the master, kill him, and enhance his own status. To prevent this from happening, secrets were revealed to the student in stages; for example a cut to the forearm may later have been revealed as a cut under the wrist which would sever both the tendons and major blood vessels. After seven or eight years' study, the student would receive his first certificate of competence, a scroll which also contained the real meanings of the techniques that he had studied up to that point.

But this was written in such a way that only he could understand them. After many years of training, students were instructed in the *okuden*, which were the secret teachings of the *ryu*.

Just before a master died he elected another to take his place, who would normally be from his own family, but if this were not possible then the honour would fall on a senior master of the *ryu*. The next grand master would then add his name to the *ryu* scrolls and perpetuate the teachings. Nearly all the *ryu* were founded because the head teacher had discovered secret knowledge through divine enlightenment, which came either during meditation or in a dream. Because of this fact most *ryu* are dedicated to a particular shrine. Katori Shinto Ryu, for example, was founded through the Katori shrine.

The methods and the weapons

The training methods of different *ryu* varied, but in general students trained in either *tandoku renshu* (alone) or *sotai renshu* (in pairs). The techniques were performed in a series of prearranged movements, called *kata*. These progressed in such a subtle way that strategy and technique eventually became intuitive and the exponent could respond to any combative situation. When training was of the *tandoku* form the exponent usually used a real weapon. However, for *sotai* training wooden weapons were substituted. The use of wooden weapons should not be underestimated. A sword of Japanese oak has the same

killing power as a steel-bladed weapon, but does not suffer the same damage as a steel weapon when struck repeatedly.

The martial arts of the samurai fell into various categories depending on the weapon used. For example, the skill of the sword became known as kenjutsu and iaijutsu. Kenjutsu dealt with techniques when the sword had already been drawn from the scabbard, for instance when it was drawn for battle and put away at the end of the day. Iaijutsu was the skill of drawing the sword on sudden encounter. When the samurai was walking along, the blade would be drawn spontaneously to deal with a sudden attack, and then put away immediately after the event.

The sword art of Kenjutsu

Kenjutsu developed in battlefield conditions and the techniques altered through the ages as armour and culture changed. In the styles of the fifteenth to seventeenth centuries part of the skill relied on finding the weak points in the armour of the samurai. Overhead cuts were often limited by the large *kabuto* (helmet) with ornate finials on either side and the techniques used to shake the blood and loose flesh from the blade were often performed in front, rather than swinging the blade over the head as adopted by the later styles. The fifteenth-century Katori Shinto Ryu style is a classic example. In *chiburi* (shaking of blood from the blade) the sword is spun on its own axis and the sword hilt struck, in order to remove any flesh that may have stuck there.

Left: *Risuke Otake* **sensei** (right with sword), *head teacher of the Tenshin Shoden Katori Shinto Ryu, trains in a fifteenth-century style with an opponent using a* **naginata** (pole arm).

Left: Otake **sensei**'s son and pupil performing kenjutsu from Katori Shinto Ryu against a **bo** (staff) attack.

Below: Early Japanese work illustrating, together with a prototype **shinai** (practice sword), a halberd and sickle and chain weapon; also armour, gloves and headgear used in kendo training.

Following pages: A demonstration of **naginata** jutsu from the Katori Shinto Ryu.

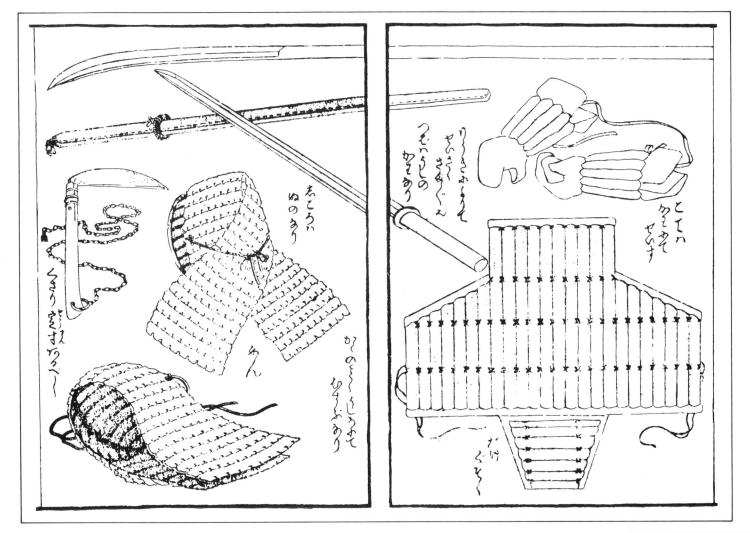

Left: *T. Danzaki* **sensei** *(right), 9th dan iaido and President of the All Japan Iaido Renmei, performing* **tachiuchi** *(sword application of iaido).*

Opposite: *There are two important shrines in Japan dedicated to warriors, and both are the founding place of many traditional* **ryu**. *Below is the Katori shrine and right (top) is the Kashima shrine.*

Below: *Otake* **sensei** *in a classical performance of iaijutsu from Katori Shinto Ryu.*

By the seventeenth and eighteenth centuries Japan was experiencing comparative peace and so tests of personal skill became more prevalent. Samurai would often draw their swords to settle a personal dispute or to engage in a challenge. With the decline of battlefield situations, the samurai was found dressed in either light armour or everyday wear and this affected the development of techniques. Vital body areas that were once guarded were now exposed and became the focal points of attack. As a result new defensive strategies developed. After an encounter the blood was often shaken from the sword by swinging it over the head in a downward flourish.

Iaijutsu — the lightning blade

Iaijutsu dealt more with everyday situations rather than those on the battlefield. No matter what style was practised, the procedure always comprised four separate parts: the drawing of the blade to meet a sudden encounter (*nukitsuke*), the cut or cuts used to despatch the enemy (*kiritsuke*), the shaking of the blood from the blade (*chiburi*), and the resheathing of the sword (*noto*). The techniques themselves dealt with many situations such as a sudden attack by several opponents, a surprise attack while bowing to someone, an enemy lying in wait behind a sliding door or an attack in a darkened room. The permutations were countless. Later in the Edo period not all styles fashioned their techniques on killing the enemy. One *ryu*, for example, only concentrated on removing the attacker's thumbs, thus making it impossible for him to hold the sword and continue. When a sword had been used in an encounter and the blood shaken from the blade, it was always wiped clean before being returned to the scabbard.

The masters and their styles

During the Sengoku era (1482-1588) many famous swordsmen established their own *ryu*. Tsukahara Bokuden (1490-1571) founded Mutekatsu Ryu, having studied both Katori Shinto Ryu and Kage Ryu. He established a great reputation by remaining undefeated in battles and challenges throughout the nation. His final philosophy rested on the ideal that the sword should only be drawn when all other peaceful means have failed. Between 1452 and 1538 the Kage Ryu was founded by Aizu Hyuga no Kami and together with Katori Shinto Ryu was one of the leading *ryu* of the era. One other style from which many other branches developed was called Itto Ryu, founded by Ito Itosai.

The Edo period saw the development of Miyamoto Musashi's style called Niten Ichi Ryu. This style made use of both the long and short swords. Few challengers ever penetrated Musashi's defence of *juji dome*, which consisted of the long and short swords crossed in front to form a wedge which offered little chance of penetration yet gave him ample opportunity for attack. One style that was strongly linked with Zen Buddhism was Yagyu Shinkage Ryu founded by Yagyu Muneyoshi (also known as Sekishusai). This *ryu* was also influenced by the teachings of the Zen priest Takuan whose philosophies leant towards the warrior. Muneyoshi was a great swordsman who served Ieyasu, who in turn became his patron. It was said that one night Muneyoshi was walking home to the village of Yagyu, when a mountain demon (*tengu*) sprang from the rocks and attacked him. In the still shadows of the moonlight, Muneyoshi drew his blade with lightning speed and blocked the demon's cut. In the same instant his returning blade severed the demon in two. The next day Muneyoshi returned to the same spot to find that he had in fact cut a large boulder in half. To this day the boulder still stands in the hills of Yagyu to bear witness to the tale.

A similar tale is told by Katori Shinto Ryu. One day a farmer's wife was killed by a wild beast. The farmer, filled with remorse and rage, took up his bow to kill the creature. When he saw it on the hillside he loosed his arrow and it struck the target. However, as he drew closer he realized that it was a rock he had hit and that the arrow was deeply embedded in a boulder. All the villagers were amazed and asked him to repeat the feat, but try as he would the arrows just bounced off the boulder. This story demonstrates that there is a power beyond present definition, that is with us in the hour of our greatest need. In times of encounter or great stress it can manifest itself and yet will not come at the bidding of man's will. In the words of Matthew Arnold, 'We cannot kindle when we will the fire which in the heart resides, the spirit bloweth and is still; In mystery our soul abides'.

Founder of the famous stick school

Not all *ryu* had the sword as their core weapon. Shindo Muso Ryu was founded by Muso Gonosuke Katsuyoshi in the late sixteenth century and had a 1.2 metre (4 ft) oak staff as its main weapon. Prior to this, Gonosuke had become a master of Katori Shinto Ryu and Kashima Shin Ryu and his favourite weapon had been the 1.8 metre (6 ft) *bo* (oak staff). One day while travelling as a *mushashugyo* (samurai who tests his skill around the country) he encountered the famous Miyamoto Musashi and challenged him to a duel. Musashi used his wooden swords (*bokken*) and defeated Gonosuke with the famous *juji dome*. He then advised the young lad not to try his skills again or the result might be fatal.

Above: *The author demonstrates the two-sword technique called* **juji dome** *that was used by Miyamoto Musashi.*

Right: *Kuroda and Shimizu* **sensei** *demonstrate techniques from Shindo Muso Ryu jojutsu.*

Left: *During a martial arts display in Kyushu two exponents demonstrate the use of stick techniques.*

Opposite above: *The **naginata** was a symbol of samurai womanhood, since it was used by them to defend the household in feudal times.*

Opposite below: *Because of its reach, the spear was a popular field weapon throughout Japan's early history.*

Gonosuke retreated to mount Homan in Kyushu where he meditated at a shrine. One night an angel in the disguise of a young boy came to him in a vision and revealed certain secret teachings. When Gonosuke awoke he devised a 1.2 metre stick which gave him greater manoeuvrability than the 1.8 metre staff, yet still kept the swordsman at bay. With his new knowledge he returned and defeated Musashi's *juji dome* in a second challenge. Musashi was so impressed at the lad's ability that he introduced him to the Kuroda clan in Kyushu, where he became the clan's head teacher of stick. Even today this is the style taught to all the police officers throughout Japan and the techniques against *juji dome* are still part of the schools' secret teachings.

Pole arms — the battlefield weapons

The *naginata* and the *yari* were both battlefield weapons which were incorporated into early *ryu* such as Katori Shinto Ryu and Ryugo Ryu. One famous exponent of *naginata* was Yoshitsune's henchman Benkei. The shaft of the early *naginata* was very long

and it was a heavy weapon, capable of cutting the horse from under a horseman or keeping the swordsman well out of cutting distance. The reverse end of the *naginata* had an iron pommel or fitting, which could strike and crush the enemy to the ground. This feared weapon was used in a sweeping action.

The *yari* would sometimes have a shaft of 4.5 metres (15 ft) or more and was carried by both footsoldiers and mounted warriors alike. The blade of the weapon varied considerably in both length and design, often having appendages for cutting and hooking. The other end of the weapon had the same type of iron pommel as the *naginata* and the blade was fitted in the same way, with a tang that was inserted into a hollow in the shaft and secured with a wooden peg. A thrust was made in a twisting action so that the triangular blade drilled its way into the wound. It was pulled out in the same manner, with the grooves preventing a suction effect which would have kept the blade trapped in the wound. The master of spear could thrust with amazing accuracy and power, while adjusting his distance and keeping the swordsman at bay.

By the seventeenth and eighteenth centuries the *naginata* and *yari* had fallen into decline, partly due to the relative peacefulness of the times. However, a short *yari* and *naginata* were often kept as weapons for household defence, the lighter more flexible *naginata* becoming a popular weapon for the women of the samurai household.

Another pole arm used by the samurai was the *tetsubo*, a long iron pole, sometimes studded along its striking area. This was not a popular weapon, but when wielded correctly by strong warriors its weight alone could crush the attacker or break open the door of an enemy stronghold. The samurai also learned the art of bojutsu, use of the 1.8 metre (6 ft) staff. Perhaps the early need for this skill arose when the head of a pole arm sheared in battle and the samurai had only the shaft left to defend himself. This is another weapon taught in the repertoire of Katori Shinto Ryu.

Weapons with chain and ball

Not all weapons developed from or for the higher ranks of samurai. During the unification of Japan under Hideyoshi, Minamoto Hidetsuna used a weapon called a *chigiriki*. This consisted of a pole and a chain with an iron weight at the end. Hidetsuna was given a special commendation by Hideyoshi during the invasion of Korea (1592-8) for his skill in battle with this weapon. He then went on to found the Araki Ryu and took the name of Araki Mujinsai. The shaft of the *chigiriki* was used to thrust, block and deflect, the chain ensnared the enemy or his weapon, and the weight broke bones or caved in the skull.

Araki Ryu had various weapons in its repertoire, one of which was the *kusarigamma*. This weapon consisted of a sickle, with a handguard part of the way along the handle. Attached was a long length of chain with a weight of approximately 1 kg (2 lbs) at the end. A similar but more sophisticated weapon was the *kusarigamma* of Isshin Ryu. This had a double-edged blade and was made of steel. The guard joined at the inner angle of the weapon and the chain was longer. The sword would often be ensnared by the chain and sometimes pulled from the warrior's hand. The sickle then sped to its target to inflict a mortal wound.

The archer and his craft

The most prominent projective weapon on the battlefield in early times was the bow and arrow. The Japanese bow took its unique shape some time before the end of the sixteenth century and was of a composite type, consisting of various cross sections of wood and bamboo. The nocking point was two-thirds of the way down and the wood was lacquered and bound. The bow length varied but each was over 2 metres (7 ft) and the composite construction altered through the different periods of Japan's history. One of the earliest schools of Japanese archery was a combative system founded about 600 years ago by Heiki Danjo and became known as Heiki Ryu.

Like most nations the early archers showered the enemy with arrows before any close encounters took place. However, Heiki Danjo developed a style of loosing the arrow with the arm straight and the string being brought back level with the shoulder, which produced greater accuracy. With the introduction of firearms the number of archers on the battlefield dropped but because kyujutsu (archery) was far more accurate than any firearm available at the time, some marksmen were retained to immobilize the key figures on the battlefield.

To defend themselves against arrow attacks the samurai sometimes used a long pole with a large ring at the top, from which hung long streamers. In the early stages of battle a samurai would hold this like an umbrella and spin it. The arrows would then be deflected by the streamers until the warrior was close enough to fight the enemy. Other defences included large portable wooden shields and *yadome* (arrow blocking). In *yadome* the samurai would use his sword to deflect any arrows which threatened him. The Maniwa Nen Ryu, attributed to the thirteenth-century monk Jion, included this training in their repertoire.

Above: Shimada **sensei** demonstrating a traditional **kata** of **naginata** against a sword. The **naginata** was a popular weapon amongst samurai women.

Weapons of the Araki Ryu founded by Araki Mujinsai in the late sixteenth century: a **chigiriki** (above), and a **kusarigamma** (below, on the right).

Left: Early Japanese warriors trained long and hard to perfect their skills with the spear and bow.

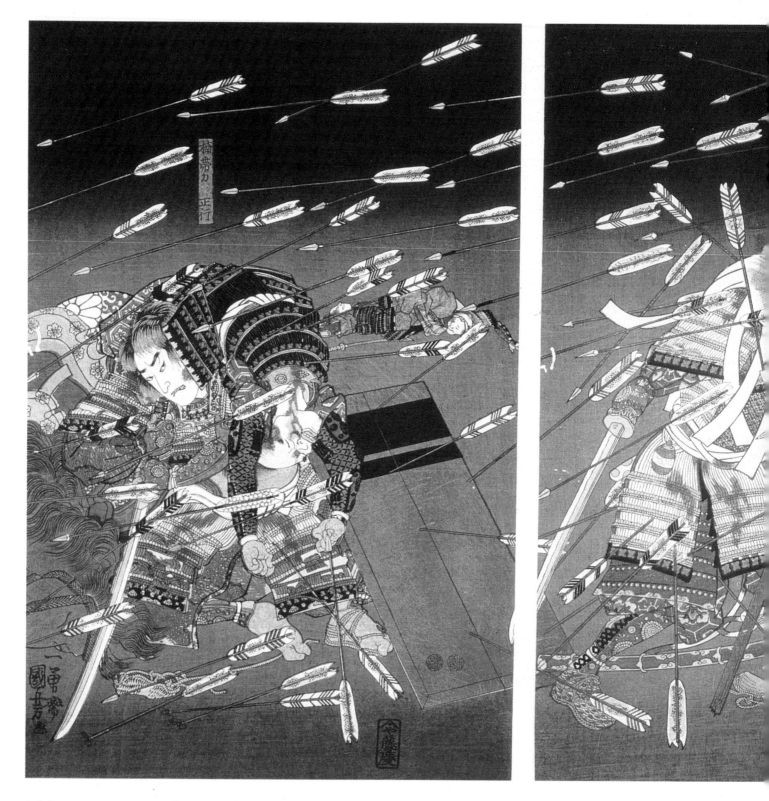

*A defence against arrows on the samurai battlefield. The streamers
were rotated and deflected the shafts of the arrows.*

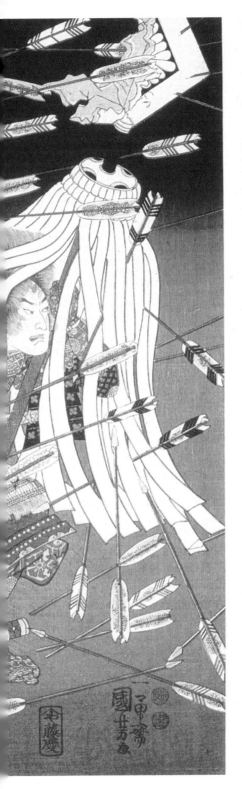

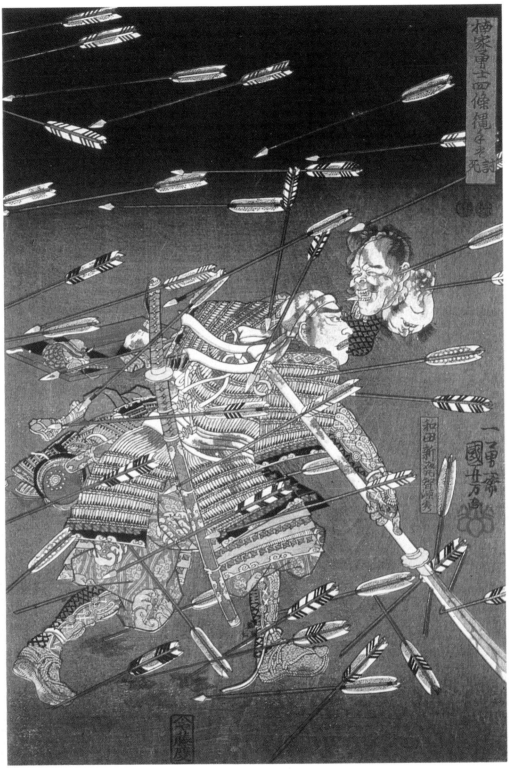

Firearms — the samurai contention

When firearms came to Japan in 1542 they not only changed the face of battle, they also introduced a new skill called hojutsu (the art of shooting). Even commoners were enlisted to use these weapons, which did not require either the bravery or skill of the samurai. By 1554 many schools, such as Shinden Ryu and Jikaku Ryu, had been established in the use of these new weapons. The arquebus or matchlock were formidable, some capable of piercing armour plate at 180 metres (200 yards). The bore of these weapons was over 2 cm ($\frac{3}{4}$ in) in diameter. Some of these firearms resembled small hand cannon. Wadding, gunpowder and ball were rammed into the barrel, then a little gunpowder was placed in the priming pan and finally the match (burning wick) was secured to the hammer (called the serpentine). If loading was carried out in the wrong order and the gunpowder was ignited by the match, the whole gun and powder pan were likely to explode. The author witnessed this very accident during a display of hojutsu in Japan in 1970.

The early firearms were often affected by rain and damp conditions but by 1830 styles such as Takashima Ryu included the use of breech-loaded weapons. Traditional training in kata (prearranged sequences) was an important part of practice; however, the firearm was never considered to be a true part of the samurai arsenal.

Empty hands — the last resort

When all else failed the samurai would resort to empty-hand tactics. However, since he was rarely without some weapon, this was often the least important aspect of his martial studies. One form of close combat, called kumi uchi (armour grappling), often involved the use of a special armour-piercing dagger called a yoroi doshi, which was thrust through a chink in the armour or, with a powerful thrust, through the plate itself. Atemi (striking a vital area) was sometimes made with the end of a pole arm or even the sword hilt. Most of the styles, such as Katori Shinto Ryu, Shinkage Ryu or Takenouchi Ryu, all have some form of grappling techniques in their syllabus.

Other skills and the samurai goal

The warrior weapons and their uses were numerous. There were iron fans, the skill of throwing steel spikes, the use of axes and many other minor arms. One important skill was bajutsu, the art of horsemanship. The samurai also learned to swim and fight underwater and to loose arrows from the water (suieijutsu), the sixteenth-century style of Shinden Ryu including this in its repertoire. To attempt to describe all the samurai weapons and kindred skills would span the pages of a large book.

The primary objective of the samurai skills was victory in combat. As a secondary consideration Confucian and Zen philosophies enhanced the practical and moral aspects. Towards the latter part of the feudal period, during the times of comparative peace, this nuance began to change. The samurai began to use their martial arts training as a means of perfecting themselves. This shift continued until the primary objective of training was self-development and the secondary ideal was victory in combat. This change continued through the Meiji era and eventually brought about the modern 'do' forms, such as judo and kendo, as we know them today. In present-day Japan the old skills of the samurai bugei (bujutsu) are still in existence as well as the modern derivations of budo.

Above left and right: *Yabusame is the spectacular skill of loosing arrows from horseback. The fast-moving steed is controlled with the feet – leaving the hands free to aim and fire.*

Opposite: *Hojutsu is the skill of firing muskets. Although accuracy was a problem, firepower changed the face of classical battlefield strategy.*

Below: *Because many old muskets are like hand cannon, exponents of hojutsu are flung violently backwards as the gun is fired, but still retain their balance and composure.*

*Leading ninjutsu master Masaaki Hatsumi
demonstrating a basic empty-hand technique. The
myths and legends that surround ninjutsu usually
have their foundation in the practical and realistic.*

9

NINJA – SHADOWS IN THE NIGHT

I n a darkened room only the flickering flame of a candle displays the grotesque dancing shadow of a ninja upon the wall. He holds a small scroll in his mouth, upon which is written a secret spell. The silence of the room is broken only by the low chant of magical incantations, as the ninja makes secret finger signs called *kuji kuri*. Suddenly his whole being begins to fade, the room is empty and silent, the shadow on the wall no longer exists, he has materialized within the walls of some distant castle.

Was this the reality of the true ninja (secret agent) or was he a flesh-and-blood human being like ourselves who played on people's magical and superstitious beliefs by using subtle tricks and illusions? Above all, the ninja were extremely practical people whose secret power, if any, was ingenuity. Unfortunately their modern-day image has been glamorized by the movie industry and become misleading. The author remembers being involved with a film director who hired a team of special forces men to act as crack troops hiding in the desert. When he came on set the desert in front of him was empty. He shouted 'get those army men here quick. I want to start shooting!' An assistant informed him that they were already there, but because they were so well camouflaged he could not see them. His reply was 'I didn't pay them for an empty desert scene. If I can't see them how can the audience. Tell them to look like they're hiding so they can be seen!'

Background of the feudal spies

The ninja spy network and strategy existed in Japan's early times, influenced by the works of Sun Tzu and other military strategists. Crown prince Shotoku Taishi (572-622) employed such people to spy and investigate the background of people involved in cases that were brought before him for judgement. Gradually the demand for spies increased and the network spread throughout Japan. Unlike the samurai the ninja were regarded as the lowest form of animal, using deceit and trickery in combat, often having no loyalty other than the fee of the highest bidder and resorting to any means available to fulfil their mission. If the ninja were captured it was certain they would be tortured, then put to death. On the other hand they were a necessary evil for the samurai because they performed the tasks that were beneath his status. Most generals, from Masashige to Yoritomo and Hideyoshi to Takeda Shingen, employed ninja to discover enemy plans and to spread subversion in their ranks. They were also used by many lords to carry out assassinations and plot intrigue. The police also employed ninja to find criminals and to investigate certain cases.

The two main styles of ninjutsu that developed throughout Japan's history were the

Left: *Apart from empty-hand techniques, the ninja learned to climb buildings and many other arts of stealth and fighting to effect their missions.*

Right: *Female ninja called* **kunoichi** *were often employed for assignments involving their feminine charms.*

Iga Ryu in the province of Mie and Koga Ryu in Shiga, both in the Osaka-Kyoto area. The network throughout Japan, however, included many other schools such as Nakagawa Ryu, Uesugi Ryu, Matsumoto Ryu, Fukushima Ryu and Bizen Ryu. Many other classical *ryu* had some aspects of ninjutsu in their repertoire, like Katori Shinto Ryu and Yagyu Ryu. During the restoration of Japan under Nobunaga, Hideyoshi and Ieyasu in the sixteenth and seventeenth centuries, Fujibayashi Nagato, Sandayu Momochi and Hattori Hanzo were leading figures of the Iga clan. Hattori Hanzo won favour with Ieyasu, who furnished his household with Iga ninja disguised as various members of staff. They acted as both bodyguards and informers for him.

The web of intrigue

The spy network of the great ninja clans reached throughout Japan. The leaders were known as *jonin*, under them came the *chunin*, and the lowest rank were called *genin*. The leaders planned the strategy, deployed the agents and collated the information. Under them the regular spies employed either specialists or expendable agents for the various tasks. There were many kinds of agents; some were 'sleepers' who were paid to continue their regular trades and keep their eyes open and act if they were ever needed. Expendable agents were often used as bait and were fed with false information or given front-line work, where their death would mean little to the skilful section of the organization. Enemy spies were employed to act as doubles and

inside agents were placed in important places to obtain information.

The plan before the plot

Before any project was undertaken it was carefully planned. If the mission was, for example, an assassination, then information about the prospective victim would have to be collated. Ninja would take up employment as staff in his household using forged references. Others would study local records and strike up acquaintances with those who knew the victim. Information on the victim's personal habits would be obtained to find out if his weakness was drink, women, gambling or the pleasure of young men. Then his favourite form of pleasure might be used to lure him to his place of execution. Some of these types of killing were simple; a woman would seduce the victim and as he slept she would thrust her hairpin into a vital point on his body. The assassination would not be detected until long after she had made her escape.

One feudal lord had no apparent vices and proved a most difficult case. He was faithful to his wife, rarely left his castle and did not drink. For over a year information was gathered with no success; then one day a ninja employed as a gardener informed the network that every morning the lord went into the garden to smell the flowers. A poisonous dust was then mixed in with the pollen and the next morning when he went to smell the flowers, he collapsed and died of asphyxiation.

A face for all seasons

The ninja studied various trades from his early youth, so that he could take on any disguise if required and remain undetected. These disguises included *shukke* (a priest), *yamabushi* (a mountain warrior), *hokashi* (a wandering singer), *shonin* (a shopkeeper), *ronin* (an unattached samurai), *chonin* (a merchant) and *hyakusho* (a farmer). When Yoshitsune was trying to escape the wrath of his brother he posed as a servant and Benkei posed as his master. At one of the many frontier posts both were stopped and their identities challenged. To protect Yoshitsune, Benkei gave his 'servant' a sound beating with a stick to allay suspicion.

The frontier post guards sometimes set cunning traps for anyone they suspected of being a ninja in disguise. Often a couple of small boys would be playing with a ball near the checkpoint gate. At a given signal from the guard the boys would throw the ball under the feet of the unsuspecting traveller. The ninja would give his presence away by instantly jumping to avoid the object, while the lazy merchant or shopkeeper would probably fall over it, or just not see it at all.

When a ninja was sent on a mission he often made contact with agents he had never met before. There were many secret codes and passwords but one code demanded special abilities. Two ninja posing as priests or musicians would meet and one would play a special tune on his *shakuhachi* (flute). The other had to match the response exactly; if he did not it meant certain death. The ninja also used signal mirrors, smoke signals, a type of semaphore and even kites.

The seen and the unseen

Most ninja led ordinary lives to cover their clandestine activities. Many were farmers who built trapdoors, escape routes and hidden rooms into their farmhouses. Sometimes the passage floor would be hinged and any stranger entering the house would fall into a pit below. False walls hid extra rooms, hidden trapdoors revealed escape passages and concealed ladders led to hideouts.

The Western image of the ninja dressed from head to toe in black is very misleading. In everyday life the ninja and his family wore ordinary clothes; the only time he would wear unusual clothes was on a stealth assignment. Black was not a good colour for night missions because it stood out. Dark brown blends more easily with the night shadows and this was the normal colour of his garments. In the snow, white clothing was worn and in rocky terrain a shade of grey; sometimes the clothing was reversible. Unlike in the movies, true ninja did not wear trousers. In fact they wore *hakama* (a traditional pleated skirt) and secured the folds around the lower legs. The *shinobizukin* was a large piece of cloth that folded around the head to cover the nose and face, this was often impregnated with an antiseptic and used as a bandage or dressing if the ninja was injured. On his feet the ninja wore *watatabi*, a kind of cotton sock, and sandals called *wara-zori*.

Left: *As well as rope, steel claws were used for climbing. Even the thick ninja swordguard provided a footing when the scabbard was placed against a wall.*

Right: *The* **shinobizuken** *was a length of cloth that the ninja bound round his head – in much the same way as Japanese warriors of the cold northern provinces used cloth to protect their heads in winter.*

Tools of the trade

On any assignment of stealth the ninja would take the minimum of equipment. If, for example, he was to assail a castle wall with a moat around it, he would use either a *mizu tsutsu*, which was a breathing tube, or *ukidaru*, which were two tubs joined by cord in which he would place his feet, then steer across with a special paddle called a *shibobigai;* or he might use another form of ninja boat. Before he left the shore he would have collected insects and birds in the area and placed them in cages around the castle. If this were not done, the silence of the animal life would alert the guards of the castle to his presence. On reaching the castle wall he could climb with the aid of padded claws called *tekage* for his hands and *ashiko* for his feet.

If a ninja were entering a mansion then he carried with him oil to silence squeaky doors. For climbing he used a *shinobikumade*, which was a collapsible bamboo pole with a rope centre; this could be pulled rigid to hook on to high walls. A *katsushiya* was a pulley that hooked on to rope so that the ninja could slide from one location to another, while *nawamusubi* was the skill of looping ordinary rope for climbing. Housebreaking tools were used for entry. *Kunai* were a selection of iron or steel levers; *tobi kunai* was a forked blade on a long pole which was used for opening the bolts on doors and gates; *kurorokagi* and *oseku* were for picking warehouse locks; and *kasugai* were iron hooks of various shapes used to secure doors to hinder any pursuers.

Once inside the premises the ninja often moved around in a handstand position, because the hands are more sensitive than the feet and so he was less likely to trip over objects or spring any traps. It was also easier to enter a small window head first and continue by handwalking. Some mansions had what were called 'nightingale floors' which squeaked as they were walked upon. These made conventional methods of stealth impossible for the ninja so if he wanted to eavesdrop on someone in the house he would sometimes use a *tsubogiri*, which was a pointed twin fork-like instrument, to drill small spyholes.

Powders and potions

The skills of pharmacy and the use of herbs were of paramount importance to the ninja and he learned how to make poisons, antidotes, explosives, knockout drugs, medicines and many other concoctions. Poisons and knockout drugs were often administered in food or drink. Sometimes a ninja posing as a musician would conceal a poison dart in his *shakuhachi*, then cover the holes up and blow the dart at his victim, who would collapse as the ninja continued to play. One multipurpose poison was taken from the blowfish, and it could be used either to paralyse or to kill. The blowfish is what some of the Japanese *sashimi* dishes are made from and only specially licensed chefs are allowed to remove its poison.

Metsubishi was the skill of blinding an attacker with powder, smoke or eye irritant. Often the powder was placed in an empty eggshell, ready to be thrown at the attacker. The ninja would blow into a special box with a mouthpiece at one end and hole at the other, a fine powder throwing up a smokescreen by which he could escape. Itching powder, snakes and small insects were also thrown at the enemy to distract him, while the ninja either fought back or escaped. With the introduction of gunpowder to Japan the ninja made primitive land mines and explosive devices. Some daggers and swords were adapted with concealed firing mechanisms and guns and cannons were added to their arsenal.

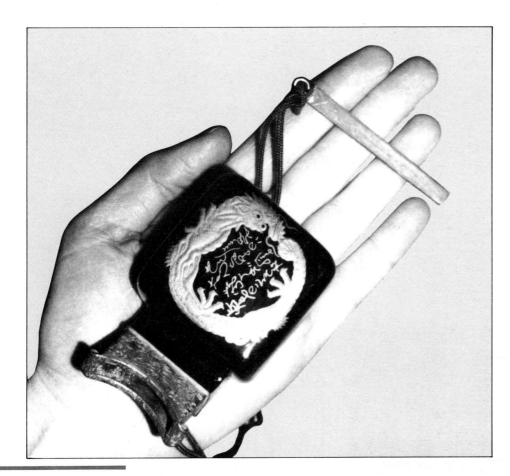

Left and below: *These unique boxes, containing dust, were used by the ninja. When blown into, they emitted a fine dust screen to blind an attacker.*

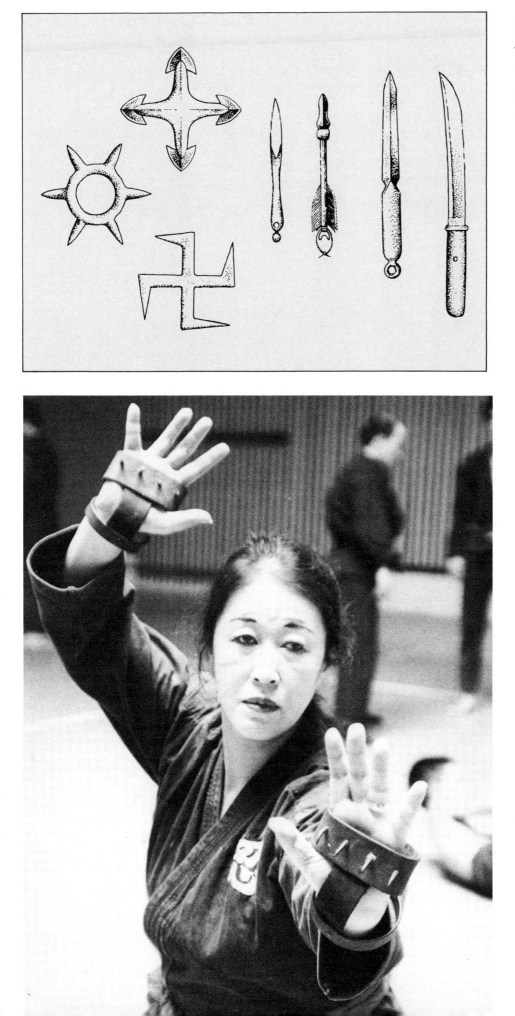

Left: *A selection of* **shuriken** *and* **shaken** *from the author's collection.*

Below left: *The wife of ninja authority Hatsumi* **sensei** *demonstrating* **tekage***, which were just as effective for defence as they were for climbing.*

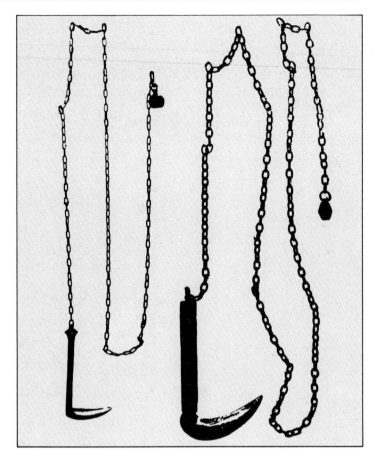

Left: The ninja **kusarigamma** *was often small enough to be concealed in his clothing.*

Right: Master Hatsumi wards off a determined attack using the keen edge of a sword blade.

Weapons of the ninja

Ninja weapons were either overt or covert, including the ninja *hankyu*, a small bow and arrow, and the ninja *kusarigamma* (called *shinobigamma*), a smaller than normal sickle and weighted chain which could be concealed in the folds of the kimono. The ninja sword (*ninjato*) was straighter than the samurai *katana*, its guard was larger and the scabbard was much longer than the blade. The *ninjato* had many applications: the guard was used to stand on when climbing low walls, the space in the scabbard often contained powder to throw in the attacker's face once the blade had been drawn, and once the false end was removed the empty scabbard became an underwater breathing tube. The *kiyoketsushiyoge* was a wooden-handled weapon consisting of a protruding spike and hook. Attached to the end of the handle was a length of chain with an iron ring on the end. Sometimes human or animal hair was substituted for the chain. In combat the chain and ring would ensnare the sword, while the hook deflected the blade and the spike killed the attacker.

There was no limit to ninja ingenuity. The *shinobizue* was an innocent-looking bamboo staff that any priest or traveller might have carried. Concealed inside the hollow of the stick might be a whole arsenal of weapons including a length of chain attached to an iron weight, a chain with a hook attached used to ensnare the enemy, and poisoned arrows. However, it was the element of surprise that enhanced the weapon's success. Other concealed weapons that the ninja used included daggers disguised as fans and rings with spikes. To prevent themselves from being followed when escaping from an assignment, *tetsubishi* were employed. These were multipointed metal spikes which the ninja dropped behind him. Pursuers invariably had to stop to pull the spikes

from their feet. Sometimes the spikes were tipped with poison — which stopped pursuit for a considerably longer period of time.

Projectiles from the hands

Shuriken, weapons thrown from the hand, fell into two main groups. The first type were *shuriken* which were straight and had only two ends, one or both of which were pointed. The second type were called *shaken* and had more than two points, often resembling a star or pointed cross. This weapon was incorporated into many classical warrior *ryu* and each design of *shuriken* was directly attributed to a particular school. The ninja were expert with this weapon. One master called Dengoro Yoshinori was a master of Shirai Ryu and could throw his *shuriken* through the centre of a hollow coin without touching its sides. He developed a style of throwing the *shuriken* while drawing his sword and cutting the enemy down.

Some *shuriken* were completely blunt and were used to stun an enemy in order to capture and interrogate him. The ninja concealed *shuriken* and *shaken* in the folds of their *hakama*. However, when they went out on a mission it was considered bad luck to carry a total of either four or seven. The last *shuriken* carried was often not thrown but used in close-quarter fighting.

The basic form of training common to most styles of shuriken jutsu was called Manji No Kata. After this form, throwing in various directions was practised. Seijo uchi was throwing from the head; gyaku uchi was throwing from the hip with the palm down; and yoko uchi was throwing from the shoulder with the palm down. Although not part of his training, in a desperate situation the ninja would extemporize *shuriken* and throw everyday objects such as plates and chopsticks.

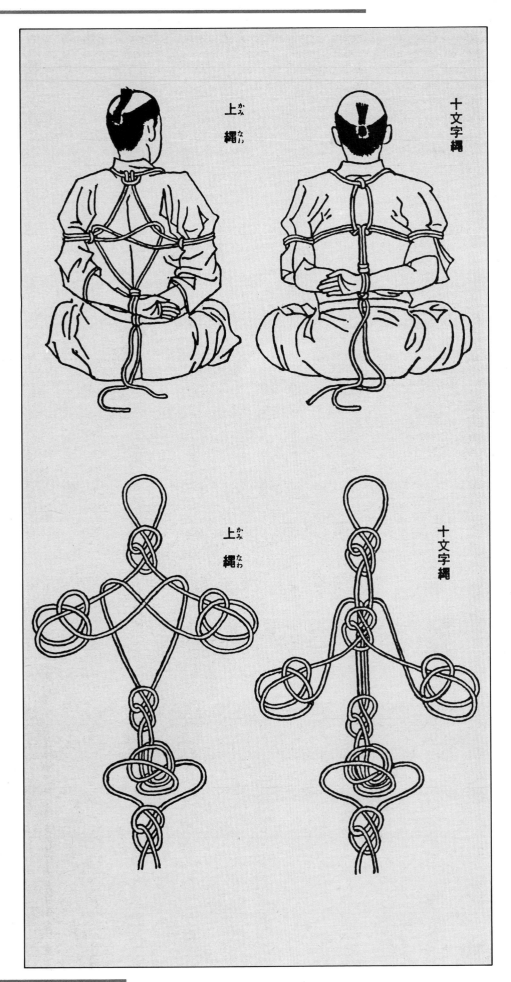

上繩

十文字繩

上繩

十文字繩

Left: *Hojojutsu is the art of restraining and tying with rope. It was a specialist skill of the feudal Japanese police officer.*

Instruction beyond endurance

Women who trained in the ninja skills were called *kunoichi*, and both men and women underwent rigorous training — even as children. Apart from learning various trades of which they could pretend to be a part, the young trainees were able to disclocate their joints at will to feign injury, escape from rope or free themselves from extremely narrow or awkward places. The last true ninja, Seiko Fujita, who died in the mid-1960s, was able to dislocate some 40 or more joints of his body and hide in extremely small enclosed areas.

Trainees learned to run vast distances, remain under water for long periods of time, jump great lengths, hang suspended from ceilings, and grip beams with their fingers and stay motionless for up to a day so that they could hide in the darkened beams of castle ceilings. Other training involved tests of endurance and strength as well as weapon and empty-hand skills. Arts involving the development of certain innate perceptions were also perfected. The ninja knew if someone was in a closed room, if a man was really asleep or if someone was stalking him. The author has seen some of these abilities in action and can confirm that the intuitive mind can with training achieve the most amazing results.

Tricks of the trade

The ninja enjoyed tricking people. Sometimes a springboard was hidden in a castle garden behind a bush, perhaps by a lower rank ninja posing as a gardener. If a master, after completing his assignment, was chased he would run to the garden, jump over the bush and leap ten or more feet in the air before disappearing over the wall. His pursuers, witnessing the amazing feat and not knowing about the concealed board, would be loath to chase him further.

One well-known ninja told a feudal lord that his power of *kiai* (focused shout) was so strong that he could even knock a bird from a tree with it. He then turned to a nearby tree and gave a great shout. To the lord's amazement a stunned bird fell from the branches. The ninja went up to it, revived it and allowed the bird to fly away. In fact the ninja had previously mesmerized a small bird which was concealed in his hand. As he shouted he threw the bird into the branches and of course it had fallen through to the ground. It was an easy matter to bring the bird out of the trance and fool the lord.

Where people were superstitious the ninja would compound their fears. One castle town had a legend that if the north gate of the castle were to move on its own, the town would be doomed. Just prior to the siege of the castle the enemy employed two ninja who hid behind the great gate. At the appropriate time they forced the gate to close without being seen. All the inhabitants were so shocked at this event that their spirit was broken and they were easily defeated.

At the flick of a switch

A great part of the ninja skill died with the advent of electricity in Japan. No longer were the dark corners of castles invisible areas for the ninja, as one click of a light switch revealed them hanging inert from ceilings. Well-lit steets and roads ended much of their activity in the shadows and modern technology thwarted their feudal ingenuity. Few people today will find any master willing to teach, or any student willing to undergo, such demanding training. Yet despite the demise of their activities — and despite Western commercial exploitation — the trade of the ninja has come down to modern times as a cultural heritage of the past, a rich mixture of classical martial skills that were used in Japan's feudal era.

Below: *Ninja authority Nawa* **sensei** *demonstrating a simple tying technique. Today the art is seldom taught – even in Japan.*

*The decisive moment – two sumo champions poised
on the knife edge of victory or defeat.*

10

GIANTS OF SUMO

T wo men of giant stature remain motionless for a moment, then in an instant their two bodies clash together. A flurry of blows are struck and blocked, throws are attempted and countered. Suddenly, like the final struggle of two mighty Goliaths, a huge human frame is thrown from the ring in which the contest began. The winner returns to the starting point of the bout, his mighty presence reflecting neither glory nor humility as he receives the certificate which testifies to his victory.

A history of giants

Sumo wrestling has a tradition in Japan that reaches back about 1,500 years, and today it is still the country's most popular spectator sport. Sumo has its roots in the national religion of Shintoism. According to tradition a great deity called Take-Mikazuchi fought a contest with the leader of a warlike tribe over the control of power. This wrestling bout not only saw Take-Mikazuchi victorious, it also laid the foundations of sumo.

There has always been close association between sumo and Shintoism. Even today the sumo ring has a roof suspended over it which resembles a Shinto shrine. In the Nara period sumo bouts were fought in the shrine precincts, along with other religious rituals, and were dedicated to the gods. As time went on the rules were formulated, customs developed and sumo began to resemble its modern-day form. This is why sumo wrestling has so much religious tradition and pageantry embroidered into each match.

Throughout early history sumo was not just restricted to ceremonial contests. Fighting men of samurai rank were also taught some use of sumo techniques for combat. Under the twelfth-century military ruler Yoshitsune the combative aspects of sumo were put to good use on the battlefield. In fact these techniques developed into certain branches of jujutsu. During the Tokugawa period in the seventeenth century a powerful samurai called Akashi remained undefeated and became the first grand champion of sumo. It was at this time that sumo developed into a spectator sport. The lower classes flocked to see great men like Akashi confront each other in the sumo ring. Akashi was reputedly 2.4 metres (8 ft) tall and was said to weigh about 180 kilos (400 lbs). In those early times it was not uncommon for bouts to end in fatality.

The eternal tradition

In modern Japan, only the sumo wrestler is still allowed to wear the top-knot which denoted samurai rank. If a sumo wrestler leaves his chosen career, the top-knot is removed during a special religious ceremony which signifies the final severing of ties with his former profession. Because of their great size sumo wrestlers rarely wear Western clothes in Japan and they can be seen walking down the street in either kimono or *ukata* (summer kimono). Whether through respect or lack of space, the public always clears a way on the pavement as they walk by.

There are perhaps no more than a thousand professional sumo wrestlers in the whole of Japan, and although many young children dream of becoming famous sumo wrestlers, few make the grade. Training is arduous. The sumo exponent has to be extremely flexible, the splits being one of his acts of flexibility. However, he must also be very strong and skilful. Westerners associate sumo wrestlers' great size with slow, clumsy movements and assume that their body bulk consists mainly of fat. Nothing could be further from the truth. The special sumo diet increases their weight, but underneath that misleading exterior is an extremely muscular body. The sumo exponent can move at great speed and has amazing power and stamina. Anyone who witnesses a training session will realize the sumo's truly awesome potential.

Prelude to an encounter

Sumo tournaments are followed as ardently as the Cup Final is in the UK or the World Series in the USA. There are six big tournaments each year, three of which are held in Tokyo. Each tournament lasts for 15 days with the lower ranks competing in the morning. As the day goes on the participating ranks get progressively higher. At the end of this period the competitors are given various ranks according to their wins. The grand champion is given the title of Yokozuna and is the only person that cannot be demoted. Next comes the rank of Ozeki, which means champion, and below him are three other ranks called Sekiwake, Komusubi and Maegashira, respectively. A Banzukc, the official ranking list, is printed in ancient-style characters and the calligraphy becomes progressively smaller with the lower ranks. These Banzuke are prized possessions for sumo followers.

Most Westerners who have seen Saturday afternoon wrestling would not at first appreciate the noble splendour of the sumo ring. But as events unfold a refreshing honesty of purpose and remarkable skill is displayed. The sumo ring is called a *dohyo* and is 4.5 metres (15 ft) in diameter at the inner circle. The overall area is 5.5 metres (18 ft) square and is raised 60 cm (2 ft) off the ground. The ring is formed by bales of straw covered with a special clay and a thin layer of sand. Surrounding the ring the spectator areas gradually slope upwards.

Below: *The giant sumo wrestlers wait with emotionless calm at the prelude to their encounter. In a few moments their huge bodies will move with cat-like agility as they battle for victory at the Tokyo Grand Championships.*

The object of a sumo bout is for one wrestler to push his opponent out of the central circle of the contest area or make him touch the floor with anything other than the soles of his feet. In modern sumo prohibited acts include punching, grabbing the loincloth covering the groin, pulling an opponent's top-knot, and kicking the stomach or chest. The loincloth worn by sumo wrestlers is called a *mawashi*. Made of thick silk, it measures about 60 cm (2 ft) wide and 9 metres (10 yds) long and is folded and then wrapped around the wrestler's middle.

Ceremonial splendour

The first event in any sumo tournament is the *dohyo-iri*, the entering ceremony. The wrestlers enter the ring in order of rank, making a very colourful and impressive sight as they parade around wearing their embroidered ceremonial aprons called *kesho mawashi*. When they leave, the reigning Yokozuna enters the contest area. He performs a special ceremony wearing a heavy thick hemp rope – weighing about 14 kilos (30 lb) – around his waist which tapers and has strips of Z-shaped paper hanging from the front. The same type of rope is often seen hanging at the entrance to Shinto shrines. The ceremony begins with the Yokozuna clapping his hands together. He then stretches his arms out horizontally and turns his palms upwards to show that he is not carrying any concealed weapons. Next he spreads his feet well apart in a low crouch and stamps down hard on the floor with alternate feet, which is a ritual for the driving away of demons from the contest area.

After the Yokozuna's ceremony the ring is entered by the *gyoji*, the referee. Wearing a samurai costume dating back in style about 500 years, he circles the ring holding a traditional fan and recites the names of the contestants in poetry form. Around the outside area of the ring the judges take up their positions and everyone awaits the beginning of the contest.

The first two contestants enter the outer circle of the contest area opposite each other and begin warming up exercises. After a pause they collect some salt and enter the inner circle to scatter it around the ring. This serves to purify the area, remove demons and protect them from injury. When they are ready they enter the inner circle and squat down facing each other, with their fists touching the ground. The referee crouches, raises his fan, the atmosphere becomes tense as they prepare to attack. After a pause they all stand up, relax and collect more salt and sprinkle it in the ring. This false start is one of many designed so that one opponent can intimidate the other with his presence. This process can last up to four minutes, or until both contestants feel that the psychological moment for the attack is right.

A flurry of action

At last the wrestlers face each other and settle. By this time there is a great deal of excitement in the audience. The referee crouches and suddenly lowers his fan. Crash, the two giants rush into each other, both huge figures moving and grappling for a hold with cat-like agility. One is almost on the edge of the circle, on the verge of stepping out. At the last moment he turns his hips under his opponent and throws him outside the contest area on to his back. Having won, he offers a friendly hand to help his opponent up and in the few minutes of total explosive action the bout is over.

When a bout is finished the exponents return to their respective sides and the winner is given a certificate by the referee.

Then the next two contestants come forward. Each bout may be brief, but it is certainly fast and furious. There are only 48 traditional throws that involve holding the *mawashi* but many other manoeuvres and variations are used. Thus it is easy to see how these applications were favoured by the samurai and how many styles of jujutsu were founded from them.

Below: In modern times only the sumo wrestler may wear the topknot denoting his samurai class. It takes a skillful attendant to ensure this unique status symbol is correctly combed and tied.

Next pages: The Shinto religion permeates the very fabric of sumo – as this early print by Kunisada portrays. Around the sumo ring are four pillars bearing the roof of a Shinto shrine, uniting the spirit of religion with the splendour of the sumo tournament.

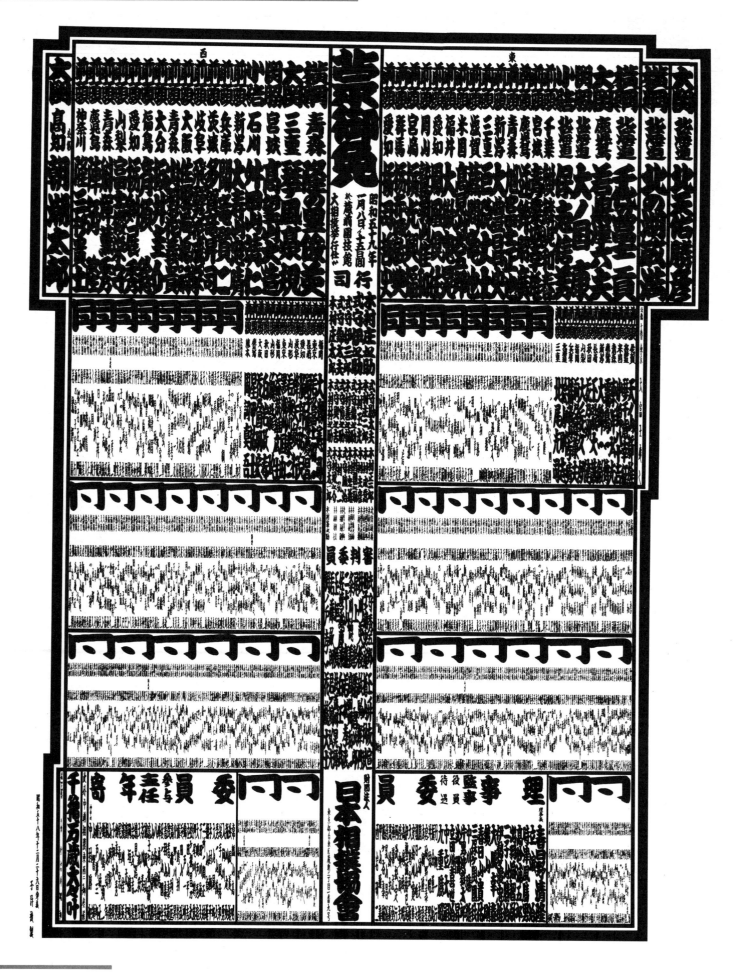

Above: *The time-span of a sumo bout is short – but the action is explosive. The referee awards the certificate of victory to the champion.*

Left: *The Banzuke is the official list of competing sumo exponents. It is presented in ancient-style Japanese calligraphy, the lettering appearing progressively smaller with the lower ranks of wrestlers. Banzuke are highly prized by fans.*

Right: *Both wrestlers strive to secure an effective technique as they grapple for a hold on their opponent's* **mawashi.**

Although jujutsu is associated with empty-hand skills, many of the traditional schools include both the use of and defence against weapons in their repertoire.

11

THE SCHOOLS OF JUJUTSU

The roots of jujutsu rest with the samurai warrior. However, the empty-hand grappling and striking techniques used by the samurai played only a secondary part compared to their weapons skills. The samurai warrior used techniques for fighting in armour called *kumi uchi* and these skills were also absorbed into many jujutsu styles. One of the earliest schools, dating back to the seventh century, was called Koden Ryu, and it would seem that much of their inspiration derived from Korea. Sumo was the earliest indigenous Japanese form of grappling and many styles, such as Takenouchi Ryu, based their techniques on the sumo repertoire. Other early styles developed empty-hand grappling techniques based on Chinese fighting traditions. The Chinese fist techniques of chuan-fa were another addition to the jujutsu repertoire and such striking became known as atemi. A great many other factors influenced the development of each style and were part of a process that took hundreds of years to mature.

Over the centuries, schools of jujutsu began to develop as separate entities to the *ryu* of the samurai class. These schools taught jujutsu, but it was also known by many other names such as yawara and kempo. It is important to realize that within the various systems many weapons were taught as well as just the empty-hand techniques. However, because the emphasis was on empty-hand skills, which often accounted for the major part of the repertoire, they became classed as empty-hand systems.

From the late Edo period many styles of jujutsu were developed by commoners, without the true military experience or martial knowledge that was inherent to the samurai class. These exponents were often employed by drinking houses and other establishments in red light districts to eject troublesome samurai and other rowdies, or to obtain money from those reluctant to pay for services rendered. By the Meiji era many jujutsu systems were available to anyone who wanted to study the skills, unlike the traditional *ryu* which selected students for their dedication, attitude and sense of moral responsibility. Because of this development, thugs used jujutsu skills for street brawls, extortion and wanton violence. Thus jujutsu gained a bad reputation in the eyes of the public – which was later to be placated by the noble ideals of judo and aikido.

Noble beginnings

One of the earliest classical *ryu* of jujutsu is Sho Sho Ryu, which was taught exclusively to the samurai from the Morioka *han* (clan). This style was derived from various other *ryu*, its early development attributed to Fujiwara Kamatari who established Koden Ryu in the seventh century. About 150 years later Saka no Ue Utamaro revised the system and called it Kazei Ryu. It was not until the time of the 27th head master of that *ryu*, Mori Uheita Kunitomo, that it became known as Sho Sho Ryu.

Like most *ryu*, skill is measured by qualifications. The student first studies the skills of Sho Sho Ryu; he then studies Kanzei Ryu which is the middle part of the system and is awarded *menkyo*. The final teachings are in Koden Ryu. Having studied those he is awarded *inka*. Within the repertoire of the collective *ryu* are the empty-hand techniques called *yawara*. Other techniques include the *bo* (1.8 metre (6ft) staff, *chotojutsu* (*naginata*) (the halberd), *hanbojutsu* (the short staff), *kenjutsu* (sword skills) and *kodachijutsu* (short sword skills).

Armour grappling of Yagyu Shingan Ryu

One traditional style that still retains the skills of the classical warrior is called Yagyu Shingan Ryu. It was founded in 1600 by a samurai called Ushu Takewaki, but the system was not completed

for several generations, until Takenaga Naoto of the Sendai *han* formulated the final *kachu kumi uchi*, which are the main skills of armour grappling. Takenaga studied Shinto Ryu, Shingan Ryu and Yagyu Shinkage Ryu and obtained the right from his teacher Yagyu Tajima no Kami to call his own style Yagyu Shingan Ryu.

When Takenaga returned to Sendai from the Yagyu area he taught the *ashigaru* (lowest samurai ranks). By this time the main repertoire was founded on *yawara* and the core techniques were *kumi uchi*. Other skills within the system included the three lengths of sword which are long, medium and short; *yoroi doshi* (armour-piercing dagger); *jutte* (iron truncheon); *tetsu ogi* (iron fan); *tanso* (short spear); *bo* (staff); *naginata* (halberd); and torinawajutsu (the skill of securing prisoners with rope). The style has been passed down to modern times and has been designated a national treasure by the Japanese government. It is one of the few styles still remaining in which the exponents wear feudal armour to effect the techniques. This is a classical jujutsu system established by samurai, for samurai.

Below: *There are many traditional Japanese scrolls that depict empty-hand strategy and restraint often used in jujustu.*

Right: *Towards the end of Japan's feudal period all classes of society began to study the skills of jujutsu.*

Takenouchi Ryu and the samurai apparition

The Takenouchi Ryu was another warrior style that placed emphasis on empty-hand skills rather than on weapons. It was founded in 1532 by a samurai called Takenouchi Hisamori. One day, on 24 June according to the secret scrolls of the *ryu,* Hisamori went to a shrine in the province of Sakushu (modern-day Okayama) where he lived. There he began his daily training. The young Hisamori loved kenjutsu and wanted to steel his fighting spirit, so he decided to train and meditate for six days and six nights. He took up his *bokken* (wooden practice sword) and made thousands of cuts against the trees to strengthen his sword skills. At night he made the *bokken* his pillow.

One night Hisamori suddenly awoke. The air was still and only a light breeze rustled the pine branches. A low mist hung over the woods and he could hear a quiet voice calling his name. Ahead of him stood a white-haired old man who seemed over 2 metres (7 ft) in stature. Although he had the appearance of a Yama Bushi (mountain warrior), this powerful-looking samurai had an unmistakable ghostly quality. Picking up his trusty *bokken*

Hisamori said 'Be gone, you cannot harm me'. The Yama Bushi replied 'I have seen you training, and because your mind is firm and your spirit is strong, I will show you one powerful jutsu technique. So let us have a match.' Hisamori did not trust his unwanted guest and when he saw an opening he attacked suddenly with his *bokken.* The Yama Bushi, without appearing to move, threw Hisamori under his knee and defeated him. When Hisamori attacked a second time he was thrown far across the woods and disarmed. Then, taking the *bokken* in his hands, the Yama Bushi broke it in two like a twig.

After this encounter Hisamori asked the Yama Bushi to teach him, and he agreed. He took the short end of the broken *bokken* and showed Hisamori *kogusoku* techniques (short sword skills), five restraining skills, and then revealed a secret teaching to him. As the sun began to rise a great wind created a dust storm, thunder filled the air and lightning tore blue flames across the sky. The image of the Yama Bushi faded and then vanished. Hisamori trained at the shrine many times after that and often the Yama Bushi would appear and reveal many secrets to him.

Below: *The short dagger, called a* **tanto,** *is here being put to use against a swordsman.*

Below: *A master of jujutsu employs an ear-piercing* **kiai** *as he disarms an opponent with a staff.*

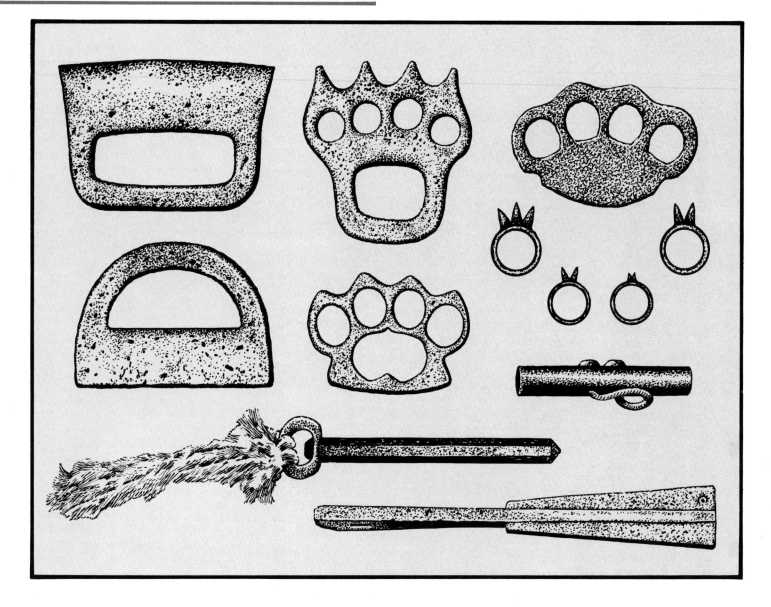

Influence of Takenouchi Ryu

The Takenouchi Ryu has influenced many other *ryu* since the time of its founder. For three generations many skills were added to the *ryu*. The second head master Hisakatsu added *shinken shobu* (a form of serious fighting competition); the third head master added *torite* (restraining techniques); and it became a complete and established *ryu*. The main skill of the style is *koshi no mawari*, which involves grappling in light armour. These sumo-like techniques are attributed to Hisamori's experiences. Other jutsu arts include *kogusoku kumi uchi* (using an armour-piercing dagger); *tori nawa* (rope tying skills); *hade* (a form of kempo); *tegasajutsu* (umbrella techniques); *shuriken jutsu* (hand-thrown weapons); *katsusatsu jutsu* (points for resuscitation or killing); *saide* (kenjutsu); *nabebuta jutsu* (saucepan lid techniques); *tessen jutsu* (iron fan skills); *iaijutsu; bojutsu; naginata jutsu; jutte jutsu; sojutsu* (spear); *kusarigamma jutsu* (sickle and chain with an iron ball); and *jojutsu* (short staff).

It was perhaps Takenouchi Ryu that marked the change in emphasis from weapons to empty-hand styles, but as time went on offshoots from this and other styles applied the principles and techniques to everyday clothing and situations outside the samurai's domain. By the end of the Edo period commoners had a

foothold in this area and trained in techniques that suited their needs. As a result of this development, many styles adapted their teachings to suit the changing times. Kito Ryu, from which the Kodokan Judo kata Koshiki no kata was formulated, modified their techniques and lost the original combative meanings.

Jujutsu without weapons

The Tenjin Shinyo Ryu, founded by Yanagi Sekizai Minamoto no Masatari at the beginning of the nineteenth century, placed great importance on *atemi* (striking techniques). Masatari was born in Seishin and from an early age studied many empty-hand styles including Shin no Shinto Ryu and Yoshin Ryu. Legend has it that one day he was attacked by over 70 thugs and sent them all running for their lives. The Tenjin Shinyo Ryu system contained 124 techniques as well as *kappo* (the skill of resuscitation), but there was little sign of the extensive weapon skills of earlier jujutsu *ryu*. Masatari eventually went to Tokyo where he established his school and changed its name to Iso Mataemon. Among the pupils of the style were the founders of both judo and aikido.

Yielding like the willow

Another style from the nineteenth century was Yoshin Ryu,

Opposite: *Many small hand weapons, similar to these, were incorporated into various jujutsu schools.*

Left: *Donn Draeger* **sensei** *employing the* **kusarigamma**, *a warrior's weapon from Isshin Ryu. However, curve-bladed* **kusarigamma** *are sometimes used in schools of jujutsu.*

which was founded by Akiyama Shirobei Yoshitoki, who had travelled for some time in China and while there, had learned various techniques in both medicine and fighting. On his return he set about formulating a comprehensive system and went to the Temmangu temple to train and meditate. One winter's day he was in the temple gardens and noticed the snow falling on the tree branches. As the branch became heavily laden with snow it snapped under the weight. Then he looked towards the lake and saw the snow falling on the supple willow tree. As each flake mounted up the willow yielded to the weight and the snow fell to the ground. From that moment Yoshitoki realized that the yielding and flexible principle was the way and that strength and resistance meant crushing defeat. Yoshitoki called his style Yoshin Ryu (willow spirit style) and formed the precepts of *ju* (suppleness and yielding).

The final transition
From the essence of the later jujutsu schools sprang the fruits of the modern 'do' forms (see Chapter 12). There were many hundreds of jujutsu styles in existence throughout Japan's late history, most of which vanished into extinction. Today only a few of the classical jujutsu styles of the warrior class exist, as do the

later schools of the common people.

One aspect worth mentioning concerns the transmission of these traditional styles to the Western world. At the turn of the century many Japanese travelled to Europe and America. They often had some experience of jujutsu styles but adapted the teachings to please Western audiences, and from that point they ceased to be the true form that existed in Japan. The author has witnessed many styles of jujutsu in the West that can be traced back to that period, but few resemble the original styles with the same names that still exist in Japan.

Modern forms of self-defence and unarmed combat that use the term jujutsu do not refer to the early styles of Japan.– they are no more than a trade name taken from the old styles. However, this does not demean their content, which must be judged case by case. Often Japanese terms are inadvertently used out of context by Western martial arts exponents who do not understand Japanese. The author recalls seeing one school of martial arts, above the entrance of which was displayed the sign 'safe self-defence and jujitsu'. Unfortunately, in larger letters above were the Japanese words 'Joroya Ryu Jujitsu', a loose translation of which is 'The Brothel School of Perfection' – a misinterpretation that no doubt gave Japanese passers-by cause for a wry smile.

A perfect judo throw just happens when total commitment is balanced with good technique and timing.

12

THE GROWTH OF MARTIAL SPORTS

The transition from the skills of the samurai to modern sports can be likened to a wet paintbrush drawn between black and white — although the two differences are clear there is still a grey area at the point of change. Rather than get involved with a grey area, let us consider the main differences. True classical martial arts were developed during Japan's feudal period for the warrior class, the emphasis being placed on victory in combat. The martial way put self-development before the practical application of techniques, while the martial sport incorporated the competitive element with that of self-development. Thus the classical martial art, the martial way, and the martial sport are three terms which define the different content of various martial skills.

Judo — the Olympic sport

Judo was one of the first martial sports to have been formulated into what became known as the 'do' system. The term 'do' means path, road or way and in this context means the path of martial arts training along which one travels to perfect oneself. Judo means the gentle or flexible way, expressing the yielding of the willow branch to the mounting snow, thus saving itself from snapping under the weight. It does not mean gentle in terms of being weak and overpowered by force.

Jigoro Kano (1860-1938), founder of Kodokan judo, was born into an era of change. At the age of seven he was witness to the restoration of the emperor Meiji to the throne and the wearing of swords by the samurai being banned. As he grew so did Japan, towards a modern government and twentieth-century technology, the feudal era diminishing into the past. In his youth Kano always suffered from bad health, so at the age of 17 he joined the Tenjin Shinyo Ryu school of jujutsu and studied under Fukuda Hachinosuke. On the death of the master Kano transferred to another style called Kito Ryu. By this time he was 21 years of age.

As Kano's health improved through his training, jujutsu itself began to decline. Due to lack of public interest and support many masters found themselves on the breadline. Some took on all-comers at public displays, others turned to crime, and some sought contracts with the police as local instructors. In the latter case there was a great deal of rivalry and often gang-style fights would take place between rival contenders for a contract. The result of these conflicts, and the decline of jujutsu itself, gave rise to the public attitude that only thugs and ruffians indulged in such base practices.

Kano knew how beneficial jujutsu training had been to him and the deep moral and social benefits that true training had to offer. So he was deeply unhappy with public opinion. He was determined to rectify this situation and, after extensive research into the many styles of jujutsu, by 1882 he established his own system, which he called Kodokan judo, and founded his first dojo (training hall) at the Eishoji temple in Tokyo. By 1887 he had brought judo to its recognizable modern form. After several moves his school finally settled at Korakuen, where it still operates today.

A graduate of Tokyo University and founder of the Japan Amateur Athletic Association, first and foremost Jigoro Kano was an educationalist. His aims were directed towards the good of society and humanity. Like the French essayist Michel de Montaigne, Kano maintained that academic and physical education should go hand in hand and not remain divided entities. His expression 'Jita Kyoei' reflects the ideal that we train half for ourselves and half for others, also that both help received and concessions made must be mutual. The author has seen many examples of the reverse of this ideal principle in Western judo, where exponents have been learning a new throw. One will attempt to perform the technique while the other will be as awkward as possible to show that he is superior in ability. When they change roles the other is equally as stubborn because he

wants his fellow pupil to experience how it feels to have an awkward partner. Neither of them are yielding, both develop hate and resentment, neither will ever learn the throw — and both will lose faith in their training. This is not Kodokan judo because it lacks the understanding of 'Jita Kyoei'.

Kodokan judo is a balance of *kata* (prearranged formal training) and competition. There are eight *kata* in judo, seven of which were devised by Kano. Nage no Kata is the form of throws; Katame no Kata is the form of holds, locks and strangles; Gonosen no Kata is the form of counters; Kime no Kata is the classical self-defence form; Itsutsu no Kata is the form of basic principles; Ju no Kata is the form of suppleness; Koshiki no Kata portrays the feudal forms of Kito Ryu; and Goshinjutsu no Kata is the form of modern self-defence which was devised after Kano's death. These formal techniques can be seen as a living textbook, by which the judo exponent may experience, develop and retain the perfect execution of the techniques. These principles are then applied in the unpredictable situation of competition.

Judo competition falls into two main categories: *randori*, a relaxed practice where the exponents try their skill, but where the winning or losing is secondary; and *shiai*, a competition where the winning counts and a referee decides the winner on points. To

Below left: *Jigoro Kano, the founder of modern Kodokan judo, whose maxim was: 'minimum effort with maximum efficiency.'*

Below right: *Judo champion Yamashita makes a decisive attack with* **uchimata** *at the Japanese championships.*

defeat your opponent in judo you must either throw him, hold him on the ground for 30 seconds (25 seconds counts as half a point), apply an armlock to the elbow, or strangle him. You cannot strike your opponent, apply a leg or head lock, or attack the face. Judo rules are comprehensive in order to protect exponents from injury.

Examinations are based on the kyu/dan system devised by Jigoro Kano. Ranking starts at 6th kyu and goes up to 1st kyu, then from 1st dan to 10th dan. In the West coloured belts denote kyu status in the order red, white, yellow, orange, green, blue and brown. In Japan white is worn till 1st kyu, and for this a brown belt is sometimes worn. From 1st dan to 5th dan a black belt is worn; from 6th dan to 8th dan the belt has red and white stripes; and from 9th dan a red belt is again worn, signifying the completion of the circle. To obtain your first black belt takes from three to five years in Japan. Few 6th dans are under the age of 40, 8th dan usually comes between 50 and 70 years of age, and 9th and 10th dans always come late in life. Early grades are based on competitive ability, knowledge of the throwing and groundwork forms, personal attitude and technical ability. The mature grades come with inner knowledge, moral and philosophical understanding, and dedication to service, where physical, moral and intellectual capacities all reach the same high level.

One of Kano's popular expressions is 'Seiryoku Zenyo', which means 'minimum effort — maximum efficiency'. People often cannot see how their energy is needlessly lost. You struggle to get into a locked car having lost your key; the locksmith comes and simply uses a bent spoon in the quarter-light. You try to get a nut off the engine of your car, pulling and pushing, heaving and struggling, the spanner slips and you hit your hand. The trained mechanic locks the spanner on and with a sharp twist the nut is free. Minimum effort and maximum efficiency applies to all things. The experienced judoka uses no effort while his opponent's is wasted. It is not only the skill but the principles that can be applied in all situations. Kano said 'once judo becomes detrimental to the health and wellbeing of the individual it is no longer my judo'. It is ideals such as these that made judo an Olympic sport.

Above: *Kotani* **sensei,** *10th dan and senior of the Kodokan in Tokyo, throwing leading British judo exponent Margo Sathaye.*

Below left: *In this judo bout, an attempt to avoid left-handed* **taiotoshi** *fails as the feet are trapped and the throw is executed.*

Below: *Matsumai* **sensei,** *head of the World Judo Federation.*

The skill of swordsmanship that developed into the sport of kendo was achieved through a process of gradual evolution.
This illustration by Kunichika reflects the era of both the sword-bearing samurai and the growth of kendo.

千代田之御表
武術
上覧

Kendo — the sword of humanity

Modern kendo has its origins in the sword skills of the samurai warrior. However, unlike judo there is no single person who can be classed as the founder. Significant changes began to occur during the Tokugawa era, although the arts of kenjutsu and iaijutsu still flourished. The comparative peace of the time brought a new concept of combat to the fore, and many exponents involved in personal encounters and tests of individual skill in duels began to make use of the *bokken* (wooden sword). This minimized fatalities to some degree, although serious injuries still often occurred. During the seventeeth century the government restricted duelling and prohibited the use of the *katana*, except under very unusual circumstances. Gradually, the various *ryu* began to find safer methods of personal encounter as well as safer training equipment.

Yagyu Ryu developed into a school of swordsmanship which enlightened the spirit while retaining the positive combativeness of the classical warrior. Many other *ryu* of that time began to place greater emphasis on spiritual development rather than on practical combative ability. As the shift in emphasis from combat to philosophy took place, so various *ryu* began to develop safe practice swords like the *fukuro shinai* which was made of bamboo and encased in soft leather. Other *ryu*, such as Maniwa Nen Ryu, devised padded headguards, wrist and chest protectors. By the late seventeenth century Onoha Itto Ryu had begun a trend in the use of safe training weapons. From this source one of its leading exponents, Nakanishi Chuta, founded a style of fencing which used protective armour and a sword made from flexible strips of bamboo. This was a major development towards kendo as we know it today.

By the mid-eighteenth century challenges in the new safer form of training were becoming popular. Strikes were made instead of cuts and the vital areas used by the classical warrior were substituted by target areas designated by the protective armour. Many samurai looked on these new skills with complete contempt. In fact they had developed with divided purpose. On the one hand competition had become a spectator sport in which *ronin* would often fight and receive a percentage of the house takings. Their motivation was usually greed and fame — even the audiences did not care about skill or higher ideals as long as there was enough violence to keep their interest. On the other hand serious exponents reached for higher ideals. They knew that beyond the need to kill lay a greater road to self-understanding and perfection. The new sword represented an instrument to reach that goal. Training was a finger pointing the way and not an end in itself.

By the Meiji era these sword competitions had become known as *gekken* (conquering sword). Rules varied and so did the equipment used; very little was standardized and bamboo swords as long as 1.8 metres (6ft) were used in bouts. Gradually, with the founding of the national martial arts centre called the Dai Nihon Butokukai in 1895, rules began to be standardized. By 1928, with the founding of the Zen Nihon Kendo Renmei (All Japan Kendo Federation), rules and equipment were uniform throughout Japan and in 1948 revisions were made to establish kendo as we know it today.

Modern kendo is divided into competitive training and *kata*. The *kata* consist of seven long-sword and three short-sword forms, which represent the techniques and values of the classical warrior. The *kamae* and strategy of these forms can be applied to competitive training. The *kata* are performed in pairs. Beginners use wooden *bokken* but skilled exponents use *katana*.

The competitive training begins with basic cutting techniques and footwork practice, which may take many months to perfect. In this type of training a *shinai* is used. This consists of four slats of bamboo with a hollow centre, one end having a leather tip and the other a leather hilt. In competition armour is worn, consisting of a chest protector called a *do*, a lower abdomen protector (*tare*), hand and wrist protectors (*kote*) and a head protector (*men*). The target areas are the centre and either side of the head, the right wrist (in some situations the left), either side of the chest protector and a thrust to the throat protector. For a cut to score it must be on target, be made with a forward slice and be accompanied by a correct step and a shout.

Like judo, kendo has a following throughout the world. Modern kendo is both a sport and a means of spiritual and moral development that promotes a positive attitude, strength of conviction, fast reactions to sudden situations and a mature attitude in society. These are some of the reasons why it is a compulsory subject for the Japanese police.

*Opposite: A modern skill called juken- do is practised in kendo armour. The exponents use wooden rifles and compete for points in bayonet fighting. However, they do not wear the **hakama**.*

Below: Viewing his opponent through the helmet of his kendo armour, the exponent has trained his mind and body for the intuitive moment in which to strike.

Left: *Many traditional styles of aikido are practised in pleated culottes called* **hakama.**

Right: *Many aikido techniques are executed from the kneeling position, called* **seiza.**

Aikido – the road to harmony

The founding ideas of aikido can be traced back to the samurai of the Aizu *han* (clan) in the Tohoku area, who studied the martial skills of various *ryu*, including Mizuno Shinto Ryu and Daido Ryu. Within these systems were empty-hand techniques called Oshikiuchi, based on the harmonious principles of *inyo (yin* and *yang)*. One of the *ryu* of the *han* was Daito Ryu which included various skills and was founded in the twelfth century by Minamoto no Yoshimitsu. It was brought to the *han* in 1574 by Takeda Kunitsugu and part of the teachings, known as aikijutsu, was passed down to Saigo Tanomo, who, in the latter part of the nineteenth century, passed his knowledge on to Takeda Sokaku, who became instructor to the Aizu warriors.

Takeda Sokaku was born on 10 October 1860 in Aizu. The family were priests by profession; however, Sokaku's father Takeda Sokichi was of *ozeki* (champion) rank in sumo, so Sokaku studied jujutsu from his grandfather. In 1870 he studied Onoha Itto Ryu under Shibuya Toma and received a teaching licence in 1876. During this period he travelled to Tokyo and studied Jikishinkage Ryu. He eventually returned to Tohoku and studied with Saigo Tanomo who taught him aikijutsu. Sokaku used his extensive knowledge to revise the system of aikijutsu within Daito Ryu and during his lifetime he taught over 30,000 students his

system of Daito Ryu aikijutsu. His pupils included the public and police throughout Japan. Of all his students only about 20 held the *menkyo* (teacher's licence), among these being Morihei Ueshiba.

Ueshiba (1883-1969) studied various martial skills and at the age of 18 he practised the jujutsu of Kito Ryu and later Tenjin Shinyo Ryu. In 1902 he joined the Yagyu Ryu school of swordsmanship and in 1908 obtained a teacher's licence. After a period in the Japanese army he met Sokaku in Hokkaido and began training in Daito Ryu. By 1917 he was awarded *menkyo*. By this time Ueshiba had begun to formulate the system that became known as aikido. It was based on the principles of harmony. The true meaning of his philosophy rests with direct experience rather than explanation. However, some insight is possible through the use of the written word. When two opposing entities meet, discord is created; when two non-opposing entities meet, harmony exists. If an opposing entity meets a non-opposing entity, it meets no resistance. In aikido the enemy's attack is absorbed by the defender who does not oppose it. The defender, however, is not defeated because in the fusion of unity between the two spirits, by yielding he has become the controlling force and directs the opponent's energy wherever he wishes.

In 1932 Ueshiba founded his *dojo* in the capital of Tokyo in the

159

area of Shinjuku, but retained his country *dojo* in Ibaraki. The master believed in universal harmony, that aikido was a means of attaining that goal and that violence and aggression could be turned aside by harmony of spirit. His repertoire of techniques included locking and throwing techniques as well as *atemi* (striking). The staff techniques represented the use of the spear, and the *bokken* reflected the principles of the sword.

Around 1928 Yoichiro Inoue began training in aikido. Later, in about 1933, Kenji Tomiki came to study with Ueshiba. He had been sent by Jigoro Kano (with whom Ueshiba had a close relationship) and was a skilled exponent of judo. Another student, Gozo Shioda, also entered Ueshiba's school at that time and in 1939 Koichi Tohei joined the *dojo*. When the master passed away in 1969 his son Kishomaru succeeded him and some of the leading masters of aikido founded their own styles. Kenji Tomiki established a sport-based aikido with elements of self-defence, Yoichiro Inoue founding a system upon similar concepts. Gozo Shioda developed a strong self-defence style and Koichi Tohei has recently introduced his style which strongly emphasizes the development of *ki* (spirit).

Right: *Kishomaru Ueshiba (left), son of the founder of aikido Morihei Ueshiba, performs a technique called* **shihonage.**

Opposite: *Morihei Ueshiba (1883-1969), the founder of modern aikido and the teacher of many leading masters.*

Below: *Aikido being practised at the Ueshiba main* **dojo***, in Tokyo.*

Ginchin Funakoshi, the father of modern karate-do.
*His **dojo** was founded in Tokyo over 50 years ago.*

Gogen Yamaguchi is known as 'the Cat' in Japan because of his masterful techniques. He modified the teachings of Gogyun Miyagi and founded the system of Goju Ryu karate.

Karate – the empty hands of truth

Karate began the transition to the 'do' form when it was introduced to Japan from Okinawa. Its founder was Ginchin Funakoshi who was born in 1868 in the capital of Shuri on the Ryukyu Islands. Funakoshi studied under various noted masters of his time in the skills of Okinawa te (see Chapter 13), including Anko Azato and master Yasutsune Itotsu, whose grip was so powerful that he could crush an adult bamboo stem with one hand. In time Funakoshi himself became a noted authority in Okinawa te and in 1922 was invited to Japan to give an official demonstration in Tokyo. Not only was this display a great success, but Jigoro Kano, the founder of judo, asked Funakoshi to lecture at the Kodokan (judo hall) on his skill. This was the turning-point in Funakoshi's career. Instead of returning to Okinawa he stayed in Tokyo to promote Okinawa te.

In the Ryukyu Islands the name Okinawa referred to the main island and apart from Okinawa te, the empty-hand styles were also called karate. The written character *kara* means China and *te* means hand. However particularly due to their past conflicts, this was not a suitable name by which to introduce a style to Japan, so Funakoshi changed the written character 'kara' to mean 'empty'; thus today karate means 'empty hand'. Funakoshi was an educated man and realized the importance of the 'do' principles. This is perhaps why he restricted Japan's early introduction to karate and left out any hint of the traditional

weapons systems that complemented the empty-hand forms. As a result of this decision modern karate has grown worldwide but the accompanying weapons systems have atrophied into almost non-existence.

Master Funakoshi found great respect through his endeavours, but this was not without some considerable cost. His wife had to remain in Okinawa and he spent his early years in Japan as a janitor and odd-job man, while teaching in his spare time. Like Ueshiba and Kano, most of Funakoshi's students were both wealthy and educated. The fame of his karate-do grew and in 1936 his *dojo* was founded in the centre of Tokyo. The *dojo* was called the Shotokan, Shoto being a pen name Funakoshi used when writing Chinese poems, and the system was named Shotokan Ryu. With the founding of the *dojo* he also incorporated the dan/kyu grading system. In 1957 master Funakoshi passed away and his son established the Shotokai on which the Japan Karate Association was founded.

Although master Funakoshi founded karate in Japan based on the modern concepts of 'do', many other styles also developed. Apart from Funakoshi's own system, the Japan Karate Association includes such styles as Wado Ryu, Goju Ryu, Shito Ryu, Rembukai and later Rengokai. One of Funakoshi's students called Kenwa Mabuni had also studied under master Itotsu and founded Shito Ryu; the Goju Ryu style was established by Gogyun Miyagi and was later modified by Gogen Yamaguchi.

One style indigenous to Japan was founded by Masutatsu Oyama, who studied Shotokan under one of Funakoshi's sons, as well as judo and boxing. Oyama was born in Korea and came to Japan when he was 16. He studied karate diligently and retreated to the mountains for more than one year's intensive training and meditation. Eventually he established his own powerful style of Kyokushinkai karate.

Despite the great variety of styles which express the numerous interpretations of karate's individuality, it is basically a system containing various forms of striking and kicking. Angular surface areas of the body, such as the toes, balls of the feet, elbows and knuckles, are used to strike at vital areas on the opponent's body. In modern times these areas have been restricted and safe techniques formalized, which are practised in *kata* form and *embu* (prearranged sparring sequences). Competition and free practice take place in some styles, the forms of which vary from school to school. The exponents of the styles that participate in competition hold either no-contact matches, in which points are scored on the ability to reach the target without hitting it, or full-contact contests, in which exponents strike each other within the safe confines of the rules of the competition.

In most styles of karate, conditioning techniques are used. Various points of the anatomy, such as the knuckles, are repeatedly struck against a special board, which kills off the sensitivity of the nerve endings and thickens the skin at that point. The skin's surface then takes on the nature of wood or steel and allows added striking and penetrating power. Often bones calcify and fuse together, causing many arthritis-like complaints in later life. However, sensible training, together with correct aftercare, can serve to avoid these dangers.

The public's image of karate is mainly one of exponents breaking a whole variety of objects ranging from planks of wood to lumps of concrete. This misleading emphasis is primarily due to public demonstrations that emphasize this aspect to excite and entertain their audiences. The true essence of karate-do is reflected in master Funakoshi's words: 'As a mirror's polished surface reflects whatever stands before it and a quiet valley carries even small sounds, so must the student of karate render his mind empty of selfishness and wickedness in an effort to react appropriately towards anything he may encounter.'

Left: *Morio Higaonna* **sensei** *is a leading master in Goju Ryu karate. The heavy weight is used for strengthening the arms and wrists.*

Right: *Competition karate allows exponents to spar in a freestyle situation.*

Below: *The iron fist of Higaonna* **sensei**, *conditioned through many years of practising striking technique on the* **makiwara**, *a straw punching post.*

Left: *Masutatsu Oyama* **sensei** *was the founder of the powerful style of karate known as Kyokushinkai.*

Opposite: *Karate* **kata** *form an essential part of traditional karate training.*

Below: *Master Konishi (left) blocking a roundhouse kick to the head.*

The massed competitors at the opening of the karate championships at the Nihon Budokan in Tokyo.

Left: *Iaido perfection: both legs and body are straight and horizontal to the ground, the blade is low after the cut, and the scabbard is correctly placed.*

Opposite page: *Nakayama Hakudo was the father of modern iaido and the last head master of Muso Shinden Ryu.*

Iaido — the steel blade of virtue

Not all modern 'do' forms are empty-hand systems, nor are they all competitive. Iaido, jodo and kyudo are examples of these forms. Techniques are practised in *kata* style, so that the individual may develop his skill and through that develop both spiritual and intuitive understanding. The result of such learning, although important, is not as valuable as the process by which that result has been achieved. This is the concept of the martial way.

Hayashizaki Jinsuke Shigenobu is regarded as the founder of modern iaido (sword drawing). He was born in Sagami (modern-day Kanagawa) in 1549. One day while meditating at the Hayashizaki shrine in Oshu he experienced a vision which led him to re-evaluate all his previous knowledge of swordsmanship. He devised a style of quick draw called battojutsu in which more emphasis was placed on self-development through training. He then toured the country teaching his new-found knowledge. Many styles were established in his name, including Shimmei Muso Ryu, Shigenobu Ryu and Hayashizaki Ryu, which was the name he took after his revelation at the shrine.

The second head master of the style, Tamiya Heibei, established his own system called Tamiya Ryu. The seventh head master Hasagawa Eishin introduced a style called Eishin Ryu, which was performed from the seated position called *tate hiza*. Omori Rokudayu Morimasa was the ninth head master and he introduced seated techniques from a position called *seiza*, which was a formal way of sitting taught by a school of etiquette called Ogasawara Ryu. By the eleventh head master there was a split in

the style and by modern times these became known as Muso Shinden Ryu and Muso Jikiden Eishin Ryu.

The last head master of Muso Shinden Ryu was Nakayama Hakudo (1869-1958) who revised and popularized the system which consisted of selected techniques from Omori Ryu, Eishin Ryu and the central teachings called Okuden. As these changes took place the skill gradually became known as iaido. Many other classical styles also assimilated their skills to encompass the higher ideals of the 'do' systems. In 1967 the All Japan Kendo Federation set up a committee of famous swordsmen from various styles and founded a system called Seitei Iaido which came under the umbrella of the organization. In 1977 another committee was set up headed by 9th dan Tomoaki Danzaki, famous student of Nakayami Hakudo and president of the All Japan Iaido Federation, under whom the author studied while in Japan. At this time the Seitei Iaido techniques were increased to ten and strict national examination standards codified. Seitei Iaido has become the standard form of iaido practised for national exams in Japan.

All iaido techniques are practised without a partner and consist of four separate actions, *Nukitsuke* is the drawing of the sword from the scabbard; *kiritsuke* is the cut or cuts used to dispatch the enemy; *chiburi* is the symbolic action of shaking the blood from the blade; and *noto* is the resheathing of the sword. Each technique represents a particular situation, for example a sudden attack from two enemies from both sides. The proper execution of these techniques constitutes a lifetime's work because there are so many fine points that must be perfected.

Left: *The sword is held above the head in Jodan Kamae. The exquisiteness of the movement reveals the beauty of good form in iaido.*

Right: *Complete mastery is required when training with a Japanese sword. One incorrect move or a split-second lack of attention could mean the loss of a thumb.*

Left: *This posture, employed in jojutsu, is
called **juji dome** and incorporates the use
of two swords.*

Right: *A demonstration of martial arts
from Kyushu, the southernmost island of
Japan.*

Jodo — the staff that guides the way

The combative stick skills of Shindo Muso Ryu have also been
formulated into a 'do' system in recent years. The last grand
master, Takaji Shimizu, was the 25th lineal descendant of the
founder Muso Gonosuke. The skills remained the secret
teachings of the Kuroda clan in Kyushu, until in 1931 Shimizu
was directed to introduce them to the Japanese nation by his
teacher Suenaga Setsu. Master Shimizu was so successful that
among his students and admirers were Nakayama Hakudo and
Jigoro Kano. In 1953 the All Japan Kendo Federation accepted
jodo under its umbrella.

The classical Shindo Muso Ryu system of '4' stick consists of
64 *kata* and 12 basic techniques, as well as a number of other
weapons which are an appendage to the style. The author, who
received personal tuition from master Shimizu, can testify that
the system is very complex and has many hidden subtleties which
were there to ensure the samurai's victory in combat. These
subtleties, however, are too subliminal for the modern man with
no classical martial arts experience so Shimizu began to formalize
a parallel system which would retain the essence of the old *ryu* but
express the modern 'do' principles.

During the author's tuition under master Shimizu in the late
1960s he witnessed the final development of Seitei Jodo. This
modern form consists of 12 basic techniques and 12 *kata*, which
are practised in pair form. All of these were drawn from the
original system, but here the combative element gave way to the
'do' principles of self-realization. This is now the accepted form of
training for national exams under the All Japan Jodo Federation.

Jodo exponents use *bokken* and *jo* (oak sword and stick). The
stick is quite capable of bending or breaking a sword blade with
one blow, thus rendering it useless. The *kata* represent various
strategies to lure the opponent into defeat and each form consists
of a number of moves. In jodo there are no secret ways to improve,
only hard work. The two most important aspects of jodo are
Seishin no Shuyo and Karada no Tanren, which constitute the
training of the mind, body and spirit as one. Correct spiritual,
mental and physical training takes the exponent to his most
skilful level, making him a trusted and useful member of society.

The way is a path to humanity

Many other classical martial art skills have reformulated their
philosophy and techniques to encompass the 'do' principles.
Naginata was brought within the control of the All Japan Kendo
Federation when a naginata section was formed in 1953.
Competition in the same format as kendo was devised with *kata*
to complement it. This system is practised mainly by women
throughout Japan. The skill of kyudo (archery) was founded in
1948 through the same channels and established as the All Japan
Kyudo Federation. Although the classical and modern systems
exist side by side, the old systems remain living history, while the
modern 'do' forms serve the higher ideals of mankind. When
these ideals cease to be reflected in the individual skills, the
principles of 'do' cease to exist and they are no longer regarded as
'do' forms.

Aspects of kyudo. Left: *The bow is drawn, and the master waits in perfect stillness until the arrow looses itself.* Right: *Part of an ancient treatise on the art.* Below: *In modern kyudo, exponents use the training as a means of self-development.*

*Seiko Suzuki **sensei** (right), 7th dan Shito Ryu Karate and 7th dan Ryukyu Kobudo, demonstrating the use of **sai** against **rokushakubo.***

13

THE FIGHTING ARTS OF RYUKYU

A t the bottom of Japan's coastline is a small chain of islands, like small tears, running towards Taiwan. The main island is called Okinawa and from this source sprang the strength and power of karate. But this was not the sole contribution of their martial skills. Because weapons were banned throughout part of their history, the islanders used everyday household tools to defend themselves, their families and their villages.

History of a village nation

The Ryukyu Islands have been inhabited for at least 2,000 years and by virtue of their strategic location have been occupied by both the Chinese and the Japanese throughout the ages. One of the earliest encounters with the Chinese was in the Sui dynasty (AD 581-618), when an expedition attempted to subjugate the islanders, who were mainly farmers and fishermen. The Japanese became aware of the islands' existence around the year 600 and by 700 had brought certain Ryukyu clans within their allegiance. In the course of time customs and beliefs from both China and Japan influenced the cultural growth of the Ryukyu inhabitants.

During the thirteenth century Okinawa was ruled by Shunten and other successive kings after him. This main island centred around village life. Each community was headed by an *aji* (from the verb *aruji*, master), who was like a chieftain, and each village community was very close knit with its own ways and customs. By the fourteenth century Okinawa was divided into three kingdoms called Chuzan, Hokuzan and Nanzan. Towards the end of the century, travellers from the Chinese province of Fukien began to settle in the area of Naha and, apart from trade links, Chinese culture again began to affect both buildings and customs alike. Although the Chuzan state instigated the Chinese relationship, the other two domains continued to seek Chinese recognition and favours. The power of the Chuzan state grew, Naha became the main trading port of the island and Shuri the seat of government. Eventually the Chuzan province became responsible for the complete control of Okinawa.

In the reign of king Sho Shin, which began in 1478, various edicts were passed. The most significant to the martial arts scholar was that which prohibited the possession or use of arms by private citizens. All implements of warfare were collected and stored in a government warehouse at Shuri. As a result of the enforcement of these edicts, not only did empty-hand fighting styles grow, but the lower classes developed fighting techniques adapting ordinary household implements and using home-made weapons that appeared to be everyday working tools.

The land that served two masters

By the sixteenth century, the Ryukyu Islands had become a focal point for trade, not only with China but also with Siam, Sumatra, Malacca and many other nations. The port of Naha was a cosmopolitan centre for all kinds of exotic and commercial goods, while the inhabitants enjoyed a wide exposure to different cultures. Although Okinawa had paid tribute to China and in return received their support, links with Japan had still been retained. During the life of Hideyoshi the islands were given to the Satsuma clan of Kyushu to govern. This, however, was in name only, since the Japanese had no claim to the islands. After the Japanese had severed diplomatic ties with China and had tried unsuccessfully to invade Korea, Hideyoshi passed on and Ieyasu took his place as shogun. It was during his rule in 1609 that an invading Japanese army, led by a *daimyo* called Shimazu Iehisa of the Satsuma clan, subjugated the islands. The king was captured and held for three years in Japan. Then, after certain pledges had been made, he was released and returned to rule.

The Ryukyu Islands now had to pay tribute to both China and Japan, as well as treating both nations as having sole sovereignty without the other's knowledge. The only advantage lay in the fact that the islands were the unofficial link through which China and Japan could communicate and trade. The Satsuma clan governed the nation and Shimazu passed a law which banned the manufacture or possession of any kind of weapon. By the late nineteenth century the Ryukyu Islands eventually fell totally under Japanese control.

With empty hands and limbs of steel

The empty-hand fighting styles of the Ryukyu islanders developed during their weapons' prohibition. Many of these systems probably came from Fukien in China and from the resident Chinese Kume communities in Naha. Among the popular names for these systems were okinawate and karate (which meant 'Chinese hand'). It was not long before the islanders modified and adapted these techniques to suit their own culture, and local names such as Shurite or Nawate began to refer to the styles that developed in those areas. The styles of Nawate and Shurite reflected the internal and external forms of Chinese boxing, respectively. Two *ryu* that existed in those times were Shorin Ryu, which perpetuated the small man's karate, and Shorei Ryu, that expressed a powerful man's ability. It is, however, unfortunate that there is almost no written record of the development of Ryukyu martial arts or the early training systems — so much is left to speculation and word of mouth.

Because the people of Okinawa were mostly farmers or fishermen, they were of hardy stock, being both strong and resilient. The close village communities made it possible for karate to be taught and be kept secret from the authorities, while the toils of labour strengthened their limbs and gave them the power to strike down even an armed attacker. Training was effected by hardening both hands and feet to penetrate wood and stone so that the aggressor could be killed with one blow. The techniques were performed only in *kata* fashion and bore traditional Okinawan names such as Naifanchi, Jitte, Jion, Chinto and Bassai. These names have been carried down to the twentieth century. The empty-hand Okinawan martial arts were eventually modified and introduced to the outside world by Ginchin Funakoshi, who was the father of modern karate.

Truth behind the hidden weapons

In the feudal period of the Ryukyu Islands, the villagers needed more than just empty-hand techniques to defend themselves. Because weapons were banned throughout part of their history, they used their own initiative to disguise weapons as innocent everyday household tools. The main weapons of the Ryukyu islanders were the *rokushakubo*, which was a 1.8 metre (6 ft) staff; the *sai*, which was a steel weapon used in pairs with a tine either side; the *tonfa*, made of wood with a handle at one end and also used in pairs; *nunchaku*, which consisted of two lengths of wood with a universal joint made of cord; *kamma*, which were farming sickles and again used in pairs; *tekko*, or knuckle-dusters; the *tinbe*, a small shield and short spear; and finally the *surujin*, which was a long weighted chain. Of these the five classical weapons are the *nunchaku, rokushakubo, sai, tonfa* and *kamma*.

Unfortunately, there is little record to prove or disprove many theories about the origin of these various weapons, but the author has heard some unusual stories that may be recounted and then discarded. The first theory involves *nunchaku*, which are said to have been adapted from rice flails. This is unlikely in their present form as flails separate the seed from the chaff; *nunchaku*, however, would pulp everything into one. One theory regarding the weapon called a *sai* is that it was originally the head of a pitchfork, which a farmer would detach from the handle when he was attacked. Obviously not a clever farmer using the shorter of two available weapons. One amazing theory concerning the *sai* expounds that one of the tines fell off and the Japanese adopted it as a weapon called a *jutte*, which is certainly untrue. There are many such innovative tales — but the truth is much more interesting.

Nunchaku — the traditional flail

There are several possible theories regarding the origin of *nunchaku*. One is that it may have derived from an instrument used for crushing beans. A second theory is that it was adapted from the instrument carried by the village night watch, which is made of two blocks of wood joined by cord. The night watch would hit the blocks of wood together to attract people's attention and then warn them about fires and protect their property. It is probable that heavy-duty weapons were made and hung with other similar farming instruments, so that they were not detected. The *nunchaku* may or may not have been joined by a chain, but it is unlikely as the Ryukyu Islands had no source of iron ore and most metals were imported. Cord was the most likely way in which they were secured together.

Unlike the exotic flailing actions portrayed in martial arts movies, the exponent of *nunchaku* was very conservative in his movements. No true exponent would spin the *nunchaku* under his legs or around his neck while his enemy was attempting to kill him. The skill was in effective blocks and instant, accurate strikes at the enemy. If the flail hit a target then it would bounce back and had to be brought within the user's control quickly. Like okinawate, nunchaku power was developed through the repetition of *kata* which developed a powerful and accurate strike. These techniques complemented the empty-hand styles.

Rokushakubo — a staff by any other name

Sticks have always been part of most nations' martial culture. They are often carried when walking and are seldom seen as a

weapon. The *rokushakubo* of Okinawa may have been introduced from China but the tapered version — called a *kon* — is indigenous to the islands. The tapered staff is about 1.8 metres (6 ft) in length, with the ends tapering considerably. The end of the *kon*, because of its reduced circumference, has greater penetrating power than the *rokushakubo* and it is not as easy to ensnare with chain weapons. The wood used is kashi or kashiwa, which is a resilient but durable type of Far Eastern oak that is quite capable of withstanding cuts from even the sharpest sword.

Rokushakubo and *kon* techniques were not designed or developed for the warrior class but for the farmers and fishermen who needed protection from footpads and brigands. The *rokushakubo* of the samurai is totally different in both technique and application. The Okinawan *kon* and *rokushakubo* rely on thrusting, swinging and striking techniques that stem from empty-hand styles of okinawate. Attacks are often avoided by agile footwork and returning strikes made at the enemy's weak points. Some of the classical *kata* that can still be seen today include Shuji, Tsukenbo, Choun and Tsukensunakake.

Above: *Motokatsu Inoue* **sensei** *(right) defends with* **sai** *against an attack by an opponent with a* **kon** *(tapered staff).*

Left: *The author Michael Finn, 4th dan Ryukyu Kobudo, training with the traditional flail — the* **nunchaku.**

181

Right: *With very few exceptions, genuine Ryukyu weapons have not so far come to the West. Here Seiko Suzuki* **sensei** *(right) shows the use of* **tonfa** *against* **rokushakubo.**

Sai — weapons from beyond the seas

Sai were not indigenous to the Ryukyu Islands. They were probably imported from China via the Fukien trade route. It is probable that in the search for arms by government officials, they did not seem like weapons among farming and fishing tools. The weapon itself has many names and is common throughout the Far East. *Sai* were used in pairs and may have been introduced to Okinawa as weapons of Chinese martial arts, then later taken and adapted by the Ryukyu styles.

The shaft and tines of the *sai* were used to block, strike and ensnare enemy weapons. Sometimes an extra *sai* was carried in the belt as a backup. The shaft of the weapon was never bladed, which would have made any reversing action in order to strike with the hilt, or block with the shaft, along the forearm, completely impossible. If the *sai* were used for thrusting to any depth into the enemy's body, because of suction it would be very difficult to withdraw the weapon, which would render it useless. This may be another reason why an extra *sai* was carried. Many of the weapons *kata* from the Ryukyu Islands were named after their founder, or their place of origin, and have been passed down to modern times. Traditional *sai kata* include Tsukenshitahaku, Kojo, Yaka and Chatanyara.

Kamma — a sickle to reap or kill

The *kamma* is an agricultural sickle and many were certainly imported from China for the farming classes. It has a long wooden handle and a thin razor-sharp curved blade at one end. It makes a formidable weapon even against the most determined enemy. Used in pairs they were flexibly reversed in the hand for both slashing and striking in a great many directions. If, however, the modern sickle resembles the ones used by the feudal farming class, it is apparent that one single blocking technique would sever the blade from the shaft and make it useless. Once again it is probable that more sturdy *kamma* were constructed for fighting — although farming ones were no doubt also used. The techniques of this weapon are not often seen in modern times and there are only two registered *kata* in Japan today, called Kanigawa and Tozan.

Tonfa — handles from a rice grinder

The *tonfa* is derived from the handles of a millstone. Once again it is probable that farmers made fighting weapons that resembled true millstone handles to such a degree that they were undetected throughout the era of weapon prohibition. The wooden handles were held, while the long shaft was swung and flailed at the attacker, then brought along the forearm to block attacks. The techniques were used in the same manner as Okinawate. For *uke* (blocking) the shafts of the *tonfa* were used along the arms; *tsuki* (punching) made use of the *tonfa* end; while *uchi* (striking) used the hinging action of the *tonfa* in the same way as that of *hiji uchi* or *empi uchi* of the empty-hand techniques. The only two listed *kata* that have come down to modern times are Hamahiga and Yaraguwa.

Offshoots of the hidden arsenal

Many of the more obscure weapons that were a part of the complete martial arts system of the Ryukyu Islands included the *sunakakebo*, which was an oar; the *sanshakubo*, a 1 metre (3 ft) staff; and the *kyushakubo*, a 3 metre (9 ft) staff. There is one

registered *kata* for the *tekko* (knuckle-dusters) called Maezato and one for the *tinbe*, which is a turtle-shell shield and short spear, called Kanigawa.

These old forms of training are protected today by the Society for the Promotion and Preservation of Ryukyu Classical Martial Arts and although there is some slight variation from teacher to teacher, the *kata* can be seen practised in their classical style. However, apart from a handful of Westerners who have trained for some years in the Far East under a recognized master, genuine Ryukyu weapons have not so far come to the Western world. This is because traditional training is too arduous, repetitive and controlled for most Western exponents. The opportunity to witness single or pairform practice of Ryukyu weapons is well worthwhile. The precision, accuracy and control of the weapon-wielding exponents reflects total judgement and mutual trust.

Below: *These primitive rice-grinding handles called* **tonfa** *show the skill and ingenuity of the Ryukyu islanders who adapted them as weapons and established this martial art.*

Left: Master Seiko Suzuki blocks with the *sai* and assumes a cat stance. The shaft and tines of this weapon were employed to block, strike and ensnare enemy weapons.

Below: Sakagami *sensei*, a leading Ryukyu Kobudo authority and karate master, adopts a stance with the **sai.**

*When exponents of shorinji kempo reach the grade of
3rd dan they are entitled to wear the robes of a priest
of the Kongo Zen sect of Buddhism.*

14

OTHER FAR EAST TRADITIONS

Most Far Eastern nations are proud of their martial traditions, each having their own foundations and developments. The Philippines, India, Malaysia, Indonesia, Korea, Borneo — and many others — each can boast of numerous weapons and empty-hand systems indigenous to their cultures. In the jungles of the more primitive Far Eastern nations, some of these martial forms are still used today in life-and-death struggles between warring tribes. Other martial arts have been refined to a greater or lesser degree and have gained popularity in other parts of the Far East — and also in the West.

Indian martial traditions

In India, the home of the Buddha, there are many forms of martial arts — just as there are many forms of religious and cultural expression. One group of martial arts studies is called Kalaripayit and is founded on Hinduism. Training is difficult in the extreme and a master will put his students through many years of arduous practice before he considers them proficient. The techniques involve both weapon and empty-hand skills, including hard punching and striking, as well as flexible grappling and locking techniques. *Lathi* and *silambam* are two forms of stick training, including the use of a short stick. Staves up to 1.8 metres (6 ft) in length are included in the repertoire. Bladed weapons used include the double-edged dagger called a *bundi*, which comes from the area of the same name. This can be used alone or in pairs, for slashing, blocking and stabbing techniques.

The Philippines — Magellan's last discovery

Hindu beliefs came to the Philippines by way of Malaysia about the time of Christ, but by the fifteenth century the islands were composed of people from China, India, Arabia and other nations who mixed with the original Negritos settlers. In the southern Philippines live a largely Muslim community called the Moro, who use an amazing range of knives in their dances and martial skills. On 6 March 1521 the Spanish explorer Magellan arrived on the shores of the Philippines. By 27 April he had been killed on the island of Mactan by the natives. His discovery of the islands brought other Spaniards, but these met great resistance from the Muslim Moro. After the Spanish occupation and the establishment of the capital in Manila, many other Western nations came to the Philippines.

In 1896 some 400,000 Tagalog people from Luzon, the largest island of the Philippines, revolted against the Spanish occupation, which led to the provisional republic in 1898. It was from this race of people that the term *kali* was derived to describe their martial arts. One of the martial skills which comes under the general term of *kali* is called arnis, which is known by other names in various provinces. This system is indigenous to the Philippines and utilizes two-bladed weapons. Training was originally carried out in total secrecy and sticks called *muton* replaced the blades for both safety and secrecy. Modern exponents use two rattan sticks up to 1 metre (3 ft) in length and techniques involve either one or two sticks in a continuous striking action against vulnerable parts of the body.

Korea and the warrior legends

During the fifth century Korea was divided into three countries: Paekche, Silla and Koguryu. After much internal conflict Koguryu defeated Paekche, but Silla obtained help from the Chinese T'ang dynasty and ruled supreme, setting up the capital in Kwangju. The noble families were well versed in martial skills and the young warriors were called *hwarang*. According to some traditions a school of martial arts was established by Won Kwang Bopsa which taught hwarangdo, a balance of philosophy and fighting arts. The system of hwarangdo paralleled the Japanese teachings of Bushido and the Korean knights became formidable and awesome warriors. Their skills included gun shin pup, which was similar to ninjutsu; kookup hwal bub, which was a form of acupuncture and medicine; nengong, which included internal and empty-hand techniques; and a weapon skills system known as way-gong. By the thirteenth century hwarangdo had fallen into decline and only the essence of these skills has been preserved today.

Through various invasions and occupations the Koreans adopted much from both China and Japan; however the empty-hand skills date back to the union of Silla and the T'ang dynasty. Chinese empty-hand fighting was taught to the *hwarang*. This system became known as t'ang-su and from this original source and with Korean influence it developed into kwonpup. Based on the skills of kwonpup, by the eighteenth century the system of tae kwon had sprung up in central Korea. In 1945 it became known as tae kwon do and has since spread throughout the world. To the untrained eye, the techniques resemble karate. However, far greater emphasis is placed on the use of kicks than punches. Among the other martial skills that have grown in popularity in recent years and which emanate from Korea is hapkido, which incorporates the use of aikido-type techniques with the kicking and striking techniques of tae kwon do.

The many skills of Indonesia

From the islands of Indonesia the Hindu-influenced skills called pentjak silat developed and with more than 150 styles in Indonesia alone there is a great variation of application. The systems include both empty-hand and weapons techniques. In particular, one weapon, called the *tjabang*, resembles the Okinawan *sai* and has been in existence from about the fifth century, the idea of the design perhaps having originated from the Hindu deity Siva. Like the *sai*, this weapon is used in pairs. The empty-hand techniques of pentjak silat include striking, locking and kicking. It is practised in both single and pair forms, a little like the Japanese *kata*. The variety of other empty-hand and weapons styles that pervade this area are so numerous as to warrant a lifetime's research.

Above: *One is never too young to begin to learn a martial art. These children in a Korean community in the USA are practising taekwondo.*

Right: *Many nations and cultures have traditional martial arts that incorporate what appear to be similar techniques, but have in fact been derived naturally and independently.*

Left: *Thailand has a long and colourful martial arts tradition. At a Thailand festival, two exponents demonstrate their skills.*

Left: *Shorinji kempo exponents, wearing the priest's robes that denote the rank of 3rd dan and above, prepare to fight at the Nihon Budokan in Tokyo.*

Nihon Shorinji Kempo — The Shaolin of Japan

Shorinji kempo was founded by Doshin So (Michiomi Nakano), who was born in 1911 in the Okayama area of Japan. When his father died he went to Manchuria and began to take an interest in Chinese martial arts. However, he returned to Japan when he was 17. Some years later, because of his previous experience, he returned to Manchuria as an intelligence agent, his cover that of a Taoist priest. During a reconnaissance mission in Peking he studied northern style Shaolin under a famous master. In 1946 he returned to Japan where he formulated a complete system on his collective knowledge and established a school of shorinji kempo in Kagawa on the island of Shikoku. This style was not registered as a martial art but as a religion that followed the Kongo Zen sect of Buddhism.

The concept of Kongo Zen is to find within the individual the true laws of nature that bind both ethical and moral values. The system is a balance of religious philosophy, technique and meditation, even *seiho* — the art of resuscitation — is taught. When exponents reach the grade of 3rd dan they are entitled to wear the robes of priesthood. Techniques can be practised alone or in pair form. Fighting sequences called *embu* are also performed. The repertoire includes punches, strikes, kicks, throws and locks.

The symbol of shorinji kempo is the swastika, which in the East is a sign of peace and universal unity. This potent symbol has its origins in early Greece as a sign of peace, and on Japanese maps the sites of most Buddhist temples are marked by a swastika. Its adoption in a clockwise form before World War II by the German National Socialist Party reflected totally reverse principles.

Today shorinji kempo has one of the biggest martial arts followings in Japan and is widely popular throughout the Far East. The author began the study of shorinji kempo in 1969 and represented Britain as the first foreigner to take part in the All Japan Shorinji Kempo Festival. It was during this period that he was introduced to the Buddhist faith, which was a prerequisite for all initiates of shorinji kempo at that time. During a public announcement at the festival, Doshin So praised the author for his efforts towards international goodwill and on his return to England the author introduced shorinji kempo to various *dojo*. Unfortunately, most onlookers and participants thought the swastika emblem reflected a Nazi movement — despite repeated affirmation of its true significance. It was not until the late 1970s that an instructor called Mizuno *sensai* was sent from Japan to Britain for the purpose of furthering shorinji kempo, and the shorinji emblem in Britain was changed to a more acceptable symbol.

Right: Murahata **sensei** demonstrating the shorinji kempo posture for meditation, called **zazen.**

Below: Master of shorinji kempo Sawada, 8th dan, defends against two attackers.

Martial traditions worldwide

In Chapter 1, a parallel was drawn between the martial arts traditions of the ancient Far East and the medieval chivalric warrior tradition that developed in the West under the influence of Christianity. Of course, similar affinities can be noticed and parallels drawn with other cultures at other times in many other parts of the world — and their description would fill a book three times as long as this one. However, one example is worth mentioning, even if briefly.

In Africa in the early part of the last century, the great Zulu ruler Shaka founded the first well-trained Zulu armies. Shaka developed their combative skills as well as the assegai, which was a flat iron spear with a wooden shaft made from a tree of the same name, which was used to great effect with the long shield. Shaka used an effective spy network, drilled remarkably well disciplined troops, used effective battle strategy and had a complete system of martial arts. The shield was used with a long spear held point down behind it, while the short spear was held in the hand for close-quarter combat. The proud Zulu race used spiritual rituals before battle to make themselves invincible and wore an amulet on the arm which they believed protected them — all reminiscent of the methods associated with the Boxer Rebellion in China.

Left: *The Zulu warriors of southern Africa employed battle strategies that were just as effective as those used by the Boxers in China – but, like the Boxers, their bravery eventually proved ineffective against modern firepower.*

Right: *Thai boxing is popular in the Far East and is gaining increasing popularity in the West. It is a martial skill that leaves little room for second place.*

*With correct training and philosophy, the real future
of martial arts lies with the world's youth.*

15

THE FUTURE OF MARTIAL ARTS

There are various aspects to be considered when speculating on the future of martial arts. The most important questions that arise are: what are martial arts? What is the purpose of such skills? Are the martial skills that have been transmitted to the Western world the same as those of the Far East? Are martial arts obsolete or do they still serve a useful purpose in society, both now and in the future? A great deal of myth and misleading information about martial arts has been perpetuated through the media, and as a result of this over-sensationalism a popular public belief about martial arts has masked the true skills that lie at the heart of these ancient and modern disciplines.

The end of violence

Martial arts and violence are not the same thing. Any form of fighting that is detrimental to both the individual and society is not a martial art. Every great master — no matter of what style — will tell you that in any confrontation, physical defence is the last resort when all other peaceful means have failed. In Japan the author has never heard any exponent say 'I learn martial arts for self-defence'. This is a Western concept. Imagine, for example, that an artist bought a paintbrush, then sat at his canvas, painting day in and day out, perfecting his artistic skills. One day his sink is blocked and he clears it with the end of the brush. It could be said that he bought the brush to clear his sink. It's the same with martial arts: although once in a lifetime such skills may be used for defence, it is not their true purpose.

From misunderstanding to deception

The fault of misunderstanding does not rest with the public alone. Many exponents of martial arts in the West believe what they read or what they are told and search no further for the truth. Many young students are enamoured by feats of amazing power and what they perceive as occult ability. The breaking of concrete blocks, housebricks, wood and tiles has a certain fascination. Breaking is a minor part of karate and some other styles but it is only practised so that the master may gauge his striking power. It is no reflection of actual ability: tiles and bricks don't fight back, they don't avoid the blow and they don't give with the force used — which is why they break.

There are two ideals associated with breaking techniques. The true exponent is modest about his achievements and is rarely seen performing in public. He sets up legitimate breaking situations only to test his skill. Unfortunately, it often takes an expert

Left: *Using body momentum and the forehead for striking, a quantity of roof tiles can be broken without resorting to trickery.*

Right: *Breaking techniques are effected with the correct use of bodyweight and mechanics.*

to tell the difference between the genuine and the bogus and in order to attract students some teachers will elaborate on their supposedly amazing superhuman ability. It is surprising how willing people are to believe what they want to be true and there are many 'tricks' that impress and entertain but they have little to do with true martial arts. Pine boards are put in an oven to dry out the water content. They do not change in appearance but break like dry twigs almost at the slightest touch. Large pebbles are smashed by an 'expert' concealing a smaller one within his closed fist, striking the large pebble with it, then letting it drop into the debris of the broken one. There are innumerable illusions of this type which distort true skills but entertain the public.

One 'master' had students believing he was an incarnation of the great Buddha. He would take all his students into a room and light a candle on a table. He would then leave the room with all his students and lock the door. From the next room he would punch in the direction of the wall in an elaborate display of 'extending psychic energy'. When the students returned to the other room, to everyone's amazement the candle flame would be extinguished. This incredible feat was achieved by an accomplice entering the room with a duplicate key when everyone had left and extinguishing the flame.

True energy or mechanical trickery?

The power of 'ki' is something that has attracted many students in recent years — that ethereal energy that flows through the body and which the initiated can 'focus' with such devastating effect that men are made to fly through the air with the pointing of a finger. That such energy exists is not denied, nor that its potential can with many years of training achieve some outstanding results. But what is all too prevalent in Western martial arts is the deception of having this power gained by subtle mechanics that go unseen by all but the trained eye. Hence many young students are captivated by a world of martial arts illusion.

Anyone can use simple mechanics, without recourse to 'ki', 'focus' — or even effort. If you ask someone to raise his arm vertically above his head then simply place your hand or finger against the wrist of the raised limb to keep it in that position, no matter how strong the person is they cannot force their raised straight arm down against your hand or finger, while you keep them in the same position with little effort at all. Another more interesting experiment is to take a wooden pole about 1 metre (3 ft) long and get someone to hold it at one end with both hands. Then take the tip at the other end with your index finger and thumb and ask them to push down with all their weight. They will be unable to force it from your grip.

There is a whole world of difference between 'ki' and mechanics. The latter can be achieved with very little practice under set conditions, but gives the same appearance as the former which takes years of training and study even to understand. Mechanical tricks can be used to prevent someone pulling you, pushing you or even lifting you. There are also mechanical techniques — all of which most readers could perform with little practice and without ever studying the martial arts — which would enable them to bend arrows and spears on the neck and to move people considerable distances with little effort.

The minds of East and West

Often the subliminal and important aspects of martial arts are lost in their transmission to the West; they are invariably adapted to suit the Western temperament rather than the Eastern philosophy being accepted by the students. Apart from self-defence, many Westerners take up martial arts to improve their 'macho' image. If the ego is fed and a belligerent, dogmatic attitude developed, then this will invariably lead to unnecessary aggression and many such 'exponents' of martial arts will look to test their 'skills' on untrained members of the public with whom they can pick an argument. One high-grade black belt teacher had an argument with a motorist, pulled his car up, jumped out and punching his fist straight through the windscreen knocked the driver unconscious. Later he bragged of his ability to his students, who thought this act established him as a true master. Most serious exponents who have such skills find no need to prove themselves in such ways. For example, the author, whilst training with the US Special Forces, met many highly-trained men skilled in combat techniques who had been forced to take life in many dangerous situations as part of their job. However, not only were they quiet, modest and thoughtful, but their interests ranged over the whole spectrum of the arts and literature. In true Eastern martial arts training the ego is the enemy from within, its growth destroys all the finer points which bring mere fighting to an art form.

Another example of East-West reverse thinking will explain the point further. Suppose you were in Japan and took a rather expensive gift to a Japanese friend's house when you visited him.

What if he took the gift from you, cast it to one side and just carried on talking to you, not even bothering to open it? It would be perfectly normal for you as a Westerner to feel slighted and even indignant. The Japanese mind would see it differently. If the host were to open the present and make a lot of fuss about it, this would mean that the gift was more important to him than your company. At a later time after you had left, he would open the gift and in due course thank you. The true future of martial arts worldwide lies in a greater understanding of East-West differences and what may be gained from this knowledge.

Teaching differences

Often Far Eastern teaching techniques are strikingly different from those in the West. In Eastern cultures, when the student wants to study a martial art he finds a teacher that he has total faith in. Then he has to prove his intent and good character in the hope that the teacher will accept him as a student. In the West the teacher advertises himself to prospective students as the best and has to convince his students of his abilities. In the East the student is in the teacher's debt, while in the West the teacher is in the student's debt for joining his class.

The Far Eastern teacher is not only critical of his new students but expects them to obey instructions without question. After all, he is the master and knows what is best — this is why the students came to him initially. The Western teacher will often not push the student to do something that he does not want to in case he leaves. He answers all questions and avoids repetition to keep interest.

Opposite: *Teaching principles for children studying martial arts in the West contrast dramatically with those of the Far East.*

Right: *Seiko Suzuki* **sensei,** *7th dan Shito Karate, passes on not only technique but also philosophy and human understanding to the children who represent the future.*

The Far Eastern teacher instructs on an intuitive plane of watch, copy and experience. He will say 'copy me' and repeat his action until the student has grasped it. He will lock or throw the student both the right and wrong way so that he can correct the student's faults by comparison. The student must take the information from the teacher and he must use his mind and body to learn. The Western teacher instructs on an intellectual plane. He explains verbally over and over again and the student does not have to think. The teacher even places the student's hands and feet in the right position. In the East the student must take his knowledge from the teacher but in the West the teacher gives knowledge to the student.

The Far Eastern teacher believes that learning is a process of trial and error and that making mistakes is part of that process. He will only point out one or perhaps two prevalent mistakes in a training session. He believes that in time the student will correct most of his own minor errors himself, but if they are constantly pointed out to him, confusion will cause the fluid, natural development of his techniques to be inhibited. The Western teacher often spends a great part of a lesson constantly pointing out error after error, sometimes not allowing time for the first errors to be corrected.

Attention to etiquette and gratitude are also important character-forming aspects of Far Eastern training. In the West many teachers allow beginners to train in street clothes or track suits until they can afford the correct kit and equipment. In the Far East the purchase of the proper kit is a sign of your commitment to train and mandatory in order to join the class. At all times kit must be clean and the student well presented. In Japan, if a student has even a frayed tape on his kendo armour he will fail his black belt exam — no matter how good his performance. Gratitude is not just bowing to everyone or the lip service of thanks. Like respect for the teacher it must come from the heart.

Right: *Kishomaru Ueshiba, the son of aikido's founder, demonstrates technique to a class at the Shinjuku dojo in Tokyo.*

Below: *A modern introduction to the martial sport of jukendo, derived from the traditional skill of bayonet fighting.*

Black belt fact and fiction

The actual costume worn by many Western martial arts exponents often personifies the diverse nature of contrasting incentives and goals compared to the Far East. Often in the West, kit of bright colours can be seen, including red, blue, green, some multi-coloured and others made from national flags. Traditional white kit is often covered with badges of all shapes and sizes, giving them a semi-official look. Belts denoting rank range through red, white, yellow, orange, green, blue, brown and black; some are also gold and silver. In the West, qualifications are given through a myriad of organizations, often each purporting to be the only official body. Black belts can be obtained in anything from a few weeks up to eight years, so diverse are the standards. While many national organizations do exist, their efforts are confounded by the struggle of the lesser bodies trying to be recognized.

In Japan the kyu/dan grade system was originated by Jigoro Kano, the founder of judo. Prior to that the martial arts schools of Japan used to issue various certificates such as *shoden, chuden* and *mokuroku, menkyo kaidan* being the highest teaching licence. In China a letter from the master stating the student's credibility and standard was sufficient. Today in Japan, apart from the classical martial arts, the kyu/dan system is universally accepted.

Examinations for judo, kendo, jodo, iaido and others are set by national bodies. The Kodokan, for example, is the leading authority for judo. For recognition by these bodies the exams must be taken in Japan. With kendo and iaido the exam is a balance of practical, theoretical and written work. Kyu grades only wear a white belt (sometimes brown), then a black belt. Coloured belts are a Western innovation. Kit has nothing on it except perhaps the student's name or one badge.

The ranks of the All Japan Kendo Federation will serve as a guide to the Far Eastern grading system. Kyu rank is from 6th to 1st kyu, when a national exam is taken for *shodan* (the first rank in black belt); this takes place three to five years after training commences. After another one year, second dan may be taken; two years after that third dan; two years later fourth dan; three years after that fifth dan may be attained; in another four years sixth dan may be taken; seventh dan comes after a five-year wait; then eight years later the exponent is eligible for eighth dan, and so forth. From third dan the exponent may teach, but true qualification is marked by a teacher's licence. The lowest teacher's licence is called *renshi* and may be taken three years after obtaining fifth dan. The next is *kyoshi* and comes after seven years as *renshi*. The highest licence is *hanshi* which is taken 20 years after *kyoshi* and the exponent must be over 55 years old.

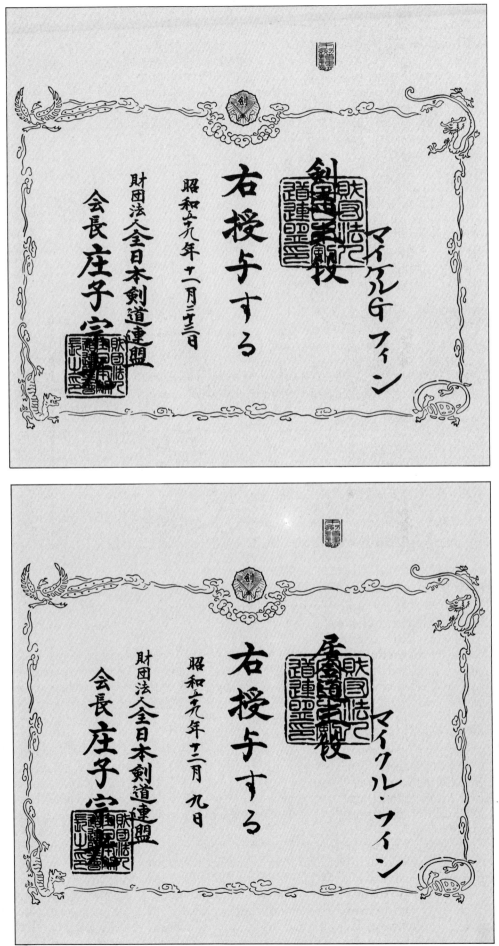

Left: *Two judo exponents struggle with total commitment as one tries to execute* **uchimata** *in a thigh throw.*

Right: *Qualifications awarded by the All Japan Kendo Federation can only be achieved in Japan. Top: The author's 3rd dan certificate in kendo issued by the Zen Nihon Kendo Renmei. Below: The author's 3rd dan certificate in iaido, issued by the Zen Nihon Iaido Renmei.*

Today — and tomorrow

The various concepts and philosophies outlined in this book can be labelled as neither right nor wrong — the fact is they exist and will continue to influence the future of martial arts. Even in past history we have seen how martial arts skills have been exploited in all nations, yet at the same time the true values of these skills were carried on to the next generation. In Hong Kong, for example, there are many new and traditional styles existing alongside each other. However, a certain number have become the domain of criminal elements. Often the old masters have all but vanished from the scene and can only be found teaching one or two students on the roof of some unassuming house. In Japan there are modern sport forms such as judo, traditional ways such as iaido, and classical systems like Katori Shinto Ryu. In many modern skills the student just walks in and joins, but the classical schools are still entered on recommendation only. Nothing, however, is perfect and even in Japan, in the less reputable systems, grades can still be bought.

In the Western world martial arts are still young and growing. Growth usually signifies change and one can only speculate as to what this youngster will become when it is a mature part of Western society. Martial arts should mean a training system for the correct development and growth of the individual, which in turn will prove of benefit to society. Without discipline, philosophy, social and moral responsibility, character-forming potential for the young exponent and stable techniques, it cannot be classed as an art form. Violence and martial arts are not the same: a true system will temper and forge the violent spirit towards a useful purpose.

Ignoring commercial exploitation, such as the sale of martial art-like street weapons and the systems that concern themselves with the growth and development of social violence, there is today more than ever a martial skill for everyone. Sports such as judo, kendo, karate, aikido and tae kwon do offer a competitive martial study that can range from an evening activity to a professional national and international level. Iaido, kyudo, jodo, tai-chi and other similar skills present another form of martial training that is not competitive but allows the individual to seek self-perfection through practice, the techniques becoming a vehicle for higher achievements. Many old classical martial systems such as Shindo Muso Ryu Jojutsu, Katori Shinto Ryu and Ryukyu Kobudo, retain the exquisiteness of historical maturity. These systems are complete, the final transition having been made from carbon to diamond, and represent a living unchanged history of the past. Those who have the dedication and patience to train in these skills will find a deep understanding of the foundations of martial arts and the spiritual values of the past.

History dictates that there will always be the unscrupulous and charlatans, lying in wait for the unsuspecting and unknowing. However, genuine teachers and legitimate organizations in most martial skills exist throughout the Western as well as the Eastern world and each must be judged on its merits. The future of martial arts is in the hands of the reader, who now knows the facts and can inform others. It is also in the hands of the students and teachers of all martial skills, who must recognize the quality of other martial skills apart from their own and help in the development of martial arts as a united whole, to serve and benefit society. The key to the future of martial arts growth lies in the Japanese character 'wa' — peace and harmony.

Right: **Hei wa** *are the Japanese characters that mean Universal Peace.*

GLOSSARY

Aikido: Martial art founded by Morihei Ueshiba and based on the use of wrist and arm locks. Used in harmony with the opponent's movement, this style is directed towards self-understanding but other later styles such as Tomiki Aikido are competitive.

Ainu: Original inhabitants of Japan. In early history they were driven north to Hokkaido and today some small communities of Ainu still live in the old traditions.

Ashigaru: Foot soldiers during Japan's feudal period. They came from the lower ranks of samurai.

Ashiko: Steel claws that fitted to the underside of the feet. Used by the ninja for climbing walls and wooden structures.

Atemi: Skill of attacking vital areas to maim or kill an opponent. The skill became popular within many styles of jujutsu and required a comprehensive knowledge of both the human anatomy and ways of striking.

Bajutsu: Japanese skill of horsemanship used by the samurai warrior. Today it may still be seen in Japan, at such events as the 'wild soma horse chase', when once a year members of samurai families put on the family armour and ride in this colourful event.

Banzuke: In sumo, formal list that gives names of all the sumo exponents in order of rank. The banzuke is a prized possession for the sumo enthusiast.

Bo: Wooden staff about 6 ft (1.8 m) in length.

Bodhidarma: Indian monk who brought Zen Buddhism to China.

Bojutsu: Skill of using a staff of about 6 ft (1.8 m) in length, usually made of Japanese oak. Bojutsu was incorporated into various Japanese ryu, but the term is also used to describe the style of 6 ft staff used in the weapon-fighting styles of the Ryuku Islands.

Bokken: Wooden Japanese sword used in the practice of sword skills, sometimes also referred to as bokken. In prearranged fighting it replaced the katana (q.v.) as a safer weapon, although sometimes the katana was also used. Apart from classical styles it is used in modern forms such as aikido.

Boxers: Chinese martial arts exponents who were part of a Shaolin temple. They trained in the martial arts but as priests and monks also followed religious teachings.

Bu: Japanese character that means martial and used in words such as bushi and budo. The actual Japanese character expresses the ideal that by training in martial skills we will become both strong and just, and violence can be averted by our presence, not our actions.

Buddhism: Religion that came from India and spread throughout the Far East. It was founded by Buddha, who died in 544 BC. The religion reveals an eight-fold path and four noble truths that show the path to enlightenment. There are many sects of Buddhism in existence today.

Budo: The martial way. It refers to the use of martial skills as a means of seeking self-perfection through training.

Bundi: Double-edged dagger from India. It is held in the fist and used for striking and cutting.

Bushi: Term that became popular in 13th-century Japan and describes the warrior class. It has a more honourable and exact meaning to describe the fighting warrior than the popular expression of samurai.

Bushido: 'The way of the warrior'. The samurai class of Japan lived by this code of ethics, much like medieval European knights. The samurai, however, placed great stress on duty and obligation to their lord or master.

Ch'iang: Chinese spear with a thick red tassel near the top of the shaft. One of the oldest weapons in the Chinese martial arts arsenal.

Cha: Chinese weapon which reesembles a steel truncheon with a tine either side of the handle. In Fukien it is called the titjio (q.v.).

Chi: Chinese word for universal energy that permeates all things. It is strong in the young and weak in the dying. It has no tangible quality but can be recognized by either its absence or its presence. In Japanese it is called ki (q.v.).

Chiburi: In the skills of iaido (q.v.) and iaijutsu (q.v.) the act of chiburi refers to the shaking of the blood from the blade after an encounter.

Chien: Traditional Chinese double-edged sword.

Chigiriki: Battlefield weapons of the lower-class samurai. Consists of a pole about 5 ft (1.5 m) long; attached to one end is a long chain with an iron weight at the end. Used in styles such as Araki Ryu, which was founded by Araki Mujinsai.

Chonin: Merchants in Japan's feudal era. One of the numerous disguises used by the ninja in their stealth operations.

Chotojutsu: Japanese art of naginata jutsu (the use of the halberd).

Chugen: Assistants to the samurai class who were not allowed to carry swords. They could be compared to the Western knight's page.

Chunin: Title given to the middle ranks within the ninja clans and network (see also jonin and genin).

Confucianism: Chinese doctrine founded by Confucius who was born about 550 BC. Its teachings placed great importance on the order of things, both within the life of the individual and within the order of society.

Daimyo: Feudal lords in Japan who often governed their own territories and estates.

Daisho: Two Japanese swords that form a matching pair. They were usually a katana (long sword) and a wakizashi (middle-length sword).

Dan: Japanese word meaning step. It is used in modern martial skills such as judo, kendo, aikido and karatedo to denote the first step in a higher level of achievement. The exponents of dan rank wear a black belt – a turning-point where true commitment begins.

Do: In kendo, the name given to the breast protector. Also the term used in scoring for the target area either side of the body.

Dohyo: In sumo, the contest area or ring where the bout takes place.

Dohyo iri: Entering ceremony at the beginning of the sumo championships. The grand champions wear special ornate aprons called kesho mawashi (q.v.).

Doshin: Lower-class police officers in Japan's feudal police force. They were only allowed to carry a short sword as a mark of their status.

Embu: Japanese term for a prearranged fighting sequence, practised to bring out some strategy and develop a natural ability when actual competition would prove too dangerous to the exponents. The word embu is used in skills such as Nihon Shorinji Kempo.

Empty-hand systems: Any martial arts system that does not use any weapons. However, in Jujutsu some weapons were used in feudal times but the main repertoire of techniques was empty hand. This is why it is also classed as an empty-hand system.

Genin: Rank given to the lower level of ninja exponents within the clan or ninja network (see also jonin and chunin).

Gi: Japanese word for kit. Also a suffix to the skill trained in. For example, a kit for karate would be called karategi, for judo a judogi, etc.

Gimu: Japanese concept of obligation, in particular the obligation a samurai had towards his lord. Even today in Japan this principle of obligation can be seen both in family life and business.

Giri: Debt of gratitude which the samurai had towards his lord. Giri and gimu are terms of mutually understood obligation. For example, in Japan the child respects his parents and will take care of them in their old age.

Go-kenin: Title similar to that of Hatamoto (q.v.) or baron. The go-kenin, however, did not enjoy quite as high a status as his counterpart.

Gumbaiuchiwa: War fan carried by generals in Japan's feudal era to direct the troops on the battlefield. Often made of iron or strong leather and consisting of a long rod with the flat fan at the end. Some fans had an amulet or talisman on them for protection.

Gyoji: Referee at the sumo championships.

Hakama: Part of the traditional clothing of the Japanese, the hakama is the lower half of the kimono (q.v.) and resembles very baggy culottes. Worn in modern times only on very special occasions. In martial arts it is still worn in very traditional skills and in some styles of aikido (q.v.).

Han: Feudal clans of the Japanese samurai.

Hanbojutsu: Japanese martial art which employs the use of a short stick of about 3 ft (1 m) in length.

Hankyu: Small version of the Japanese bow used by feudal ninja for both assassination and sending messages. Sometimes it would be used to launch incendiary devices.

Hanshi: Highest form of teacher's licence for martial arts in Japan. It can only be taken after the teacher has held the rank of kyoshi (q.v.) for 20 years and he must be over 55. In reality most hanshi are in their 70s and usually about 8th dan. The qualification can be gained only in Japan.

Hapkido: Korean martial art that incorporates the techniques of both taekwondo (q.v.) and aikido (q.v.).

Harakiri: Means belly cutting. It is an impolite expression for the act of traditional Japanese suicide known as seppuku (q.v.), but popularly used by Westerners to describe this act.

Hard styles: Martial arts systems that express power to effect their purpose. Although there is soft in hard and hard in soft, these styles predominate with strength and self-motivating energy to effect their purpose. See also Soft styles.

Hatamoto: Samurai who owned their own estates during Japan's feudal period. They acted as commanders in battle.

Hojutsu: With the introduction of firearms to Japan in 1542, the skill of hojutsu grew. It is the art of firing old muskets and during the time of Ieyasu soon began to replace the archer on the battlefield. The art has been preserved and can still be seen in modern times.

Hokashi: A wandering singer from Japan's feudal era. One of the many disguises used by the ninja.

Honbu: Japanese term for any martial arts headquarters.

Horimono: Carved or etched motif, sometimes a dragon, on the blade of some Japanese swords. In the feudal era some swordsmiths would use such a design to cover up a fault or blemish in the blade.

Hsing i: Internal Chinese style of martial arts attributed to Yueh Fei in the late Han dynasty. More linear in movement than tai chi (q.v.) but also founded on Taoist principles.

Hwarang: Name given to feudal warriors from Korea, later used to denote the martial skill, hence hwarangdo.

I-Ching: Ancient Chinese Book of Changes. It contains the eight trigrams (q.v.), which are symbols that stem from yin yang (q.v.) and can be altered to represent all the various combinations of existence. Today the I-Ching is often used for fortune telling.

Iaido: Japanese skill of sword drawing. Considered to be a martial way because unlike iaijutsu (q.v.), where the priority was victory in combat, iaido uses the skills as a vehicle for finding self-perfection and understanding.

Iaijutsu: Sword art of the samurai class which involves drawing the sword from the scabbard as quickly as possible to deal with a sudden encounter. Iaijutsu refers to the feudal samurai skills; the modern forms come under the heading of iaido (q.v.).

Inyo: Japanese name for yin yang (q.v.).

Ji samurai: Samurai who came from the farming classes; country gentry.

Jito: Japan's 12th-century land stewards, appointed by the shogun to keep order.

Jitte: (See jutte).

Jo: Staff of Japanese oak, about 4 ft (1.2 m) in length.

Jodo: Modern style of stick fighting using a 4 ft (1.2 m) stick. In Japan it was founded by the All Japan Kendo Association and is called Seitei Jodo. The system was developed from a traditional style called Shindo Muso Ryu. Jodo's aim is towards self-perfection.

Jonin: Rank given to the head of a ninja clan (see also chunin and genin).

Ju: Japanese term for gentle or soft. However, it should not be confused with weak. Soft refers to flexible or yielding, of turning your opponent's force against him by yielding and using it to your advantage.

Judo: Japanese martial art and Olympic sport. Professor Jigoro Kano was the founder of modern Kodokan judo, established in 1882. In the repertoire exponents may compete using throws, holds, locks and strangles.

Judoka: Student of judo. When the suffix 'ka' is added to any Japanese martial skill the term means an exponent or student of that skill. Thus a student of kendo is a kendoka and of aikido, an aikidoka, etc.

Juji dome: Sword technique. The famous Japanese swordsman Miyamoto Musashi used this technique, which means 'cross stop'. He crossed both the long and short sword in front of him in the form of a narrow 'x', a very strong position from which to face an encounter.

Jujutsu: Japanese term that means the flexible art and referring to the feudal empty-hand systems of fighting (although weapons were sometimes used). In the West it is often used to describe modern self-defence techniques and is sometimes referred to as jujitsu.

Jukendo: Modern Japanese martial sport based on the concepts of bayonet fighting. Exponents wear armour much like in kendo (q.v.), except that zabuton (trousers) and not hakama (q.v.) are worn. A wooden rifle with a rubber tip is used to execute the thrusting and blocking techniques.

Jutte: Iron truncheon with a single tine at one side. The weapon is indigenous to Japan and was often carried by the lower class feudal police, who were not allowed to carry swords. Also called jitte.

Jutte jutsu: Art of using the jutte (q.v.). The tine was used to trap a sword blade, while the aggressor was restrained.

Kabuto: Helmet of the samurai warrior. Sometimes quite ornate, the style of helmet worn by the armour-clad samurai often denoted rank and many famous generals were known by their particular kabuto design.

Kaishaku: The act of cutting off the head during seppuku (q.v.). When a samurai had to commit seppuku he needed the help of a special person who would cut off his head, called a kaishakunin.

Kalaripayit: Generic term for a collective martial system of Indian origin based on Hinduism.

Kamae: Japanese word meaning posture. In martial arts it is used to describe both the combative and sporting postures taken while training, but the samurai used kamae as a chess master uses the pieces on the board. Often a samurai took up a kamae that left no opening to attack.

Kamma: Simple agricultural sickles used for defence by the farming class of both Japan and the Ryukyu Islands. They are regarded as one of the five main classical weapons of the Ryukyu Islands, which include rokushakubo, sai, nunchaku and tonfa. Kamma were used in pairs.

Kanji: Chinese characters used by the Japanese since early times. The Japanese language is made up of kanji; hiragana, which are simple characters used in a phonetic manner; and katakana, which are also phonetic characters used for foreign words.

Kappo: Art of resuscitation used by some members of the warrior class in feudal Japan.

Karate do: Japanese martial art. There are many styles of karate do. The original skill came from the Ryuku Islands and was brought to Japan by Ginchin Funakoshi in the early 20th century. The repertoire of techniques includes punching, striking and kicking. The do form is a means of self-development.

Kashin: Relatives of the daimyo (q.v.) in Japan's feudal period who were given land and acted as retainers to the daimyo.

Kasugai: Iron hooks used by the ninja of feudal Japan to secure doors and stop their pursuers chasing them.

Kata: Prearranged forms of training in Japanese martial arts that are like a living text book. They contain all the fundamental information, in animate form, with which to perfect technique and understanding of the particular skill.

Katana: Japanese curved sword carried by the samurai class. It was tucked into the belt, on the left side of the body, with the cutting edge facing upwards. Apart from being a weapon of war, katana were works of art, forged from pure steel.

Katsu: Form of resuscitation used by the samurai in certain combative styles. It is little practised today but is still a part of the traditional curriculum in Kodokan judo.

Katsusatsu jutsu: Art of studying the vital points of the body that can be used to both kill and cure.

Katsushiya: Pully that hooked over rope. The feudal ninja used it to slide from one roof to another. This type of housebreaking instrument is still used today by many modern military organisations such as the special forces.

Ken: Japanese term for sword. It is usually used as a prefix to words such as kendo, meaning sword way, or kenjutsu, meaning sword art.

Kendo: Modern Japanese skill of swordsmanship, founded on the samurai traditions. The exponents wear protective armour and use a bamboo sword to compete against each other.

Kenjutsu: Means sword art and is the Japanese skill of swordsmanship using the already drawn sword to deal with an encounter. Kenjutsu refers to the classical sword skills that were developed during Japan's feudal era.

Kesho mawashi: Ornate aprons worn by sumo grand champions at the beginning of the sumo championships, during the initial opening parade.

Ki: Japanese for life force. In Chinese it is called chi and in India it is known as prana. A vigorous and healthy person is said to have a strong flow of the life force within them. In a sick person the life force is weak. The flow of life force may be improved with healthy activity and a healthy mind.

Kiai: Japanese word for the shout used in martial arts. The skill can be used in various ways. In combat the kiai was used to cause the attacker to either freeze or be distracted long enough to gain the victory. The kiai comes from the stomach.

Kimono: Traditional costume of Japan worn by both men and women. The man's Kimono is made up of a long-sleeved jacket and baggy trousers called hakama (q.v.). Over the jacket a coat called a haori is worn, on which is the family crest. Popular men's colours are black and brown.

Kiritsuke: In the arts of both iaido (q.v.) and iaijutsu (q.v.), the word refers to the cut or cuts that are used to despatch the enemy.

Kiyoketsushiyoge: Ninja weapon consisting of a short handle, with a hook and spike protruding from it. Attached to the other end is a length of rope or chain, with a ring secured on it.

Koans: Poems used in Zen philosophy to bring about a state of enlightenment. In Japan's 12th and 13th centuries, special warrior koans were introduced for the samurai class, called Kamakura koans.

Kodachijutsu: Feudal skill of using the short Japanese sword in combat. The word means short sword art.

Kodokan: Meaning a place for studying the martial ways but refers specifically to the headquarters of judo in Tokyo, founded in 1882 by Jigoro Kano and known as the Mecca of world judo.

Komono: Commoners appointed to help the feudal police force in Japan. They were not allowed to carry swords and often used only a jutte (q.v.).

Kon: Staff 6 ft (1.8 m) in length which is tapered at both ends. Used in the classical martial art styles of the Ryukyu Islands. Both the kon and the rokushakubo (q.v.) were used by the islanders.

Kondei: Noblemen who in 8th-century Japan were trained in military skills. They were at the disposal of the state in times of war or civil trouble.

Kote: Name used in kendo to describe the gauntlets worn with the armour. It is also the term used to describe the scoring area of the wrist. However, in kendo it is usually only a cut to the right wrist which scores.

Kuji kuri: Series of hand movements and hand positions used by the ninja, often together with a chant. The purpose of this ritual is steeped in mysticism, but apart from its occult aspects, it was performed on a mission in times of stress to restore confidence.

Kumi uchi: Feudal Japanese skill of grappling in armour. When the samurai fought in armour at close quarters, special techniques were used to defeat the enemy. These included the art of drawing a short dagger and plunging it into a weak point on the armour.

Kunai: Types of iron levers used by feudal ninja for housebreaking.

Kung-fu: Cantonese word which means 'an acquired skill' and can refer to any artistic ability. In recent years it has been used as a collective term to describe Chinese martial arts.

Kung pang: Chinese weapon consisting of a simple long wooden pole used in traditional weapon systems.

Kunoichi: Female ninja who were trained to use not only their ninja skills but also their feminine charms.

Kurokagi: Lock-picking instruments used by the ninja of feudal Japan.

Kusarigamma: Weapon consisting of a sickle, which has a length of chain and a weight attached to it. Often incorporated an iron guard to protect the hands. It was a weapon used by farmers, low-ranking samurai and ninja. It was employed by styles such as Araki and Isshin Ryu.

Kwan tao: Halberd used in Chinese martial arts, dating back to before the Han dynasty and used on the battlefield.

Kyoshi: Middle level of teacher's licence in Japan for martial arts. It is attained only after the teacher has held the lower status of renshi (q.v.) for 7 years and he must be over the age of 31. It can be attained only in Japan.

Kyu: Japanese word that means class or grade. It denotes students below the rank of black belt. In judo in Japan, for example, there are seven kyu grades before black. In the West coloured belts denote kyu rank, but in Japan only the white belt is worn.

Kyudo: Modern skill of Japanese archery. Unlike the old art of kyujutsu (q.v.), where the samurai's priority was an accurate arrow to despatch the enemy, modern kyudo exponents use the skill as a means of seeking self-perfection and is considered a martial way.

Kyujutsu: Classical Japanese archery, in which the warrior used a combative style. The Japanese bow is very long, with the nocking point about two-thirds of the way down. Ancient kyujutsu techniques have been adapted for a form of self-development called kyudo (q.v.).

Kyushakubo: Staff of about 9 ft (2.5 m) in length used in martial arts of the Ryukyu Islands. In Japan is very close to the skill of using the spear.

Lathi: Form of Indian martial art using various lengths of stick.

Machi bugyo: City commissioners in Japan's feudal era, who acted as magistrates and heads of the police forces.

Makiwara: Straw punching pad used in karate, often mounted on a flexible wooden post or wall. The exponent punches and kicks it repeatedly to harden the striking areas of the hands and feet.

Mawashi: Loincloth worn by sumo wrestlers.

Meakashi: Commoners employed by the feudal Japanese police to perform menial and risky tasks.

Men: Head protector in kendo, which incorporates a steel grille at the front and heavily padded area for the rest of the head. It is also the name for a cut to the centre of the head. A cut to either side of the head is called yoko men.

Menkyo: Licence or certificate of proficiency given to exponents of various classical Japanese ryu as proof of their ability within the school.

Metsubishi: Skill employed by the ninja of feudal Japan of using some kind of powder or liquid to blind an attacker and allow either escape or to gain an advantage in combat.

Mizu tsutsu: Breathing tube, often made from hollow bamboo, used by the ninja for breathing under water. Sometimes the ninja sword scabbard had a removable end and was used for the same purpose.

Mushashugyu: Samurai who had studied under one master and attained a high level of competence. When the time was right they travelled throughout Japan, visited other styles and put their knowledge into practice. Gaining this wide spectrum of experience enhanced their skills.

Muton: Sticks used in the Philippine martial art of arnis. The muton replaced the blades that were originally used.

Nabebuta jutsu: Art of defence using a saucepan lid. It is not a common martial skill and is included in the style of Takenouchi Ryu.

Nagimaki: Japanese halberd with a very long blade and a short handle. This type of weapon dates back to very early times.

Naginata: Japanese halberd, consisting of a long shaft with a curved blade at one end and an iron pommel at the other. It was a battlefield weapon which later became popular with women of the samurai households.

Naginata do: Martial sport derived from the art of naginata jutsu. Today exponents use a halberd consisting of a wooden shaft and bamboo blade. They wear armour and compete much like in kendo, except that the legs are also a target. In Japan it is a very popular sport among women.

Nawamusubi: Ninja term for looping rope in a special manner for climbing and stealth operations.

Ninja: Japanese feudal assassins and exponents of stealth who often acted as spies or secret agents. In the Western world the ninja are often confused with the commercial image that has been created by film and television.

Ninjato: Sword used by the ninja of feudal Japan. It had a shorter blade than the katana (q.v.) worn by the samurai, the sword guard was thicker and heavier, and the scabbard was used to conceal useful objects. It was a multipurpose weapon used in ninjutsu.

Noto: Skills of both iaido (q.v.) and iaijutsu (q.v.), the word noto referring to the returning of the sword to the scabbard after the encounter is complete.

Nukitsuke: In the art of iaido (q.v.) and iaijutsu (q.v.), nukitsuke describes the actual act of drawing the blade from the scabbard on sudden encounter.

Nunchaku: Weapon from the Ryukyu Islands consisting of two lengths of wood joined by cord. Because weapons were banned through part of their history, many inhabitants of the Ryukyu Islands defended themselves with everyday items. One theory is that the nunchaku derived from bean crushers.

Okappiki: Menial casual helpers appointed from commoners to help the Japanese feudal police.

Okinawa te: Traditional empty-hand fighting skill of the people of Okinawa. It was used in the feudal era for self-protection; in modern times it was introduced to the mainland of Japan and developed into the sport of karate do (q.v.). Original styles, however, still exist today.

Okuden: In the classical Japanese martial arts the teachings of various styles were layered. The outer layer was sometimes called shoden, the middle was chuden, and the secret inner teachings were called okuden.

Oseku: Lock-picking instruments used by the ninja of feudal Japan.

Pa-kua: Internal Chinese martial art style attributed to Tung Hai Ch'uan during the Ch'ing dynasty and like tai-chi and hsing-i it is a soft form founded on Taoism. Its principles are based on the eight Pa-Kua trigrams and the teaching of the I-Ching.

Pentjak silat: Hindu influenced martial skill from Indonesia embracing many styles. The system includes both weapon and empty-hand techniques.

Prana: Indian word often used in yoga to describe the life force (see also chi and ki).

Randori: Form of training used in modern martial skills such as judo and some styles of aikido. It is a 'free practice' where two exponents fight within the rules, but emphasis is placed on development of the skill rather than winning.

Renshi: Lowest grade in Japan of teacher's licence. It cannot be attained until the exponent has held the rank of 5th dan for 3 years, the exam can only be taken in Japan, and it entitles the teacher to be recognised on a national level.

Rokushakubo: This 6 ft (1.8 m) staff, usually made of Japanese oak, was used in both Japan and the Ryukyu Islands during the feudal era.

Ronin: Samurai who for some reason or another were masterless. If a lord had his land confiscated by the crown or lost his estate in the course of civil conflict, all his samurai became masterless and roamed the country seeking employment.

Roundhouse: Circular kick or strike used in karate. A roundhouse kick is one that comes out in a crescent movement to the side.

Ryu: Japanese word referring to a school of combative study in the martial arts. Many ryu had one core weapon, but studied others to build up a battlefield repertoire. Strategy and field fortification were among other subjects often studied.

Sai: Weapon from the Ryukyu Islands consisting of a metal rod with a tine either side; used in pairs and complementing the empty-hand systems of Okinawa te. It is thought that they came to the islands through the Fukien trade route, during the early feudal period.

Saide: Another term to describe kenjutsu (q.v.).

Sake: Japanese rice wine either fermented or distilled and a national drink popular during the feudal era. Today, however, the modern Japanese often favour whisky over traditional sake.

Samurai: Popular word to describe the warrior class of Japan (see also Bushi). It is derived from the Japanese verb sameru which means to serve.

San cha: Chinese weapon consisting of a trident mounted on a long pole. It may have originated from agricultural implements.

San chet kwon: Martial arts weapon of China, consisting of three sections of staff each being about 3 ft (1 m) long and all joined by a universal joint.

Sanshakubo: Staff of 3 ft (1 m) length used in martial arts of both the Ryukyu Islands and Japan.

Sasumata: Long pole with a fork shape at the end used by the feudal Japanese police to restrain violent criminals by trapping the neck or limbs.

Seiza: Popular Japanese formal manner of sitting, the two legs being folded under the body and the back held straight. It is a manner of sitting in most Japanese martial skills.

Sensei: A literal translation of the word means teacher; however, in Japan it is used in martial arts to denote teachers from the rank of 3rd dan and above. In the West it is used as a mark of respect for any black belt.

Seppuku: Polite term for the act of disembowlment, when the samurai had to commit suicide as an act of bravery or of punishment. It was made illegal during the Meiji Restoration in 1867. The last noted figure to take his life in this way was the author Yukio Mishima in the 1970s.

Shaken: Multi-pointed or round throwing instruments used in Japan's feudal era. They were thrown from the hand and were used by both the samurai and the ninja.

Shiai, meaning competition, is a term used in modern Japanese skills such as judo and kendo where both exponents compete within the framework of the rules to gain a victory.

Shinai: Bamboo sword used in kendo. It consists of four slats of bamboo between 36 to 39 inches in length. At one end there is a leather tip and at the other a hilt of leather. A string marks the back of the blade and a sword guard of leather or plastic protects the hilt.

Shinobigamma: Sickle and chain with a weighted end used by the feudal ninja. It differed from the warrior's weapon because it was smaller and could be concealed in the kimono.

Shinobikumade: Housebreaking tool used by the ninja for climbing. It consists of a segmented bamboo pole with a rope running through the centre and a hook at one end. The ninja lifted it rigid to place the hook over the point of entry, then climbed up the loose segmented sections.

Shinobizue: Bamboo pole used by Japan's feudal ninja because it looked like an ordinary walking staff. Inside, however, there was a chain and weight (or hook). Sometimes the other end concealed a lead weight which gave the innocent-looking weapon combative advantage.

Shinobizukin: Large piece of dark cloth the ninja used to bind around their head and cover their face. The cloth also acted as a dressing if the ninja was injured; prior to wearing it the cloth was treated with an antiseptic solution.

Shintoism: National religion of Japan, founded through the birth of the islands when the deities Izanagi and Izanami withdrew a lance from the sea and the drops that fell back formed the islands of Japan. It includes the belief that each emperor descended from Amaterasu the sun goddess.

Shishi: Group of Japanese extremists who supported the emperor but hated the shogun in Japan's 19th century. The Shishi took part in acts of terrorism and assassination during that period.

Shogun: Supreme military ruler of feudal Japan, answerable only to the emperor. There were many great shogun, the first being Yoritomo who ruled from Kamakura in the 13th century.

Shonin: Shopkeeper in Japan's feudal era and one of the many disguises assumed by the ninja.

Shorinji kempo: Japanese word that means temple boxing; in Chinese it is pronounced shaolin. Nihon Shorinji Kempo is the Japanese style founded on Chinese tradition by Doshin So. It encompasses both technique and religious philosophy in the form of the Kongo Zen sect of Buddhism.

Shugo: Feudal Japanese constables of the 12th century who were appointed by the shogun to keep order.

Shukke: A priest. The ninja of Japan's feudal era often used this disguise when on assignments.

Shuriken: Straight throwing weapons used during Japan's feudal era. They were either single or double pointed and were thrown from the hand. Today even in Japan there are only a few genuine exponents of this skill.

Silambam: Indian martial skill using various lengths of stick.

Sodegarami: Instrument used by the feudal police of Japan to restrain violent criminals. It was a long barbed pole that ensnared the sleeves of the kimono and restricted the attacker's movement.

Soft styles: Martial arts systems that are yielding in nature. Often the enemy's energy is absorbed or redirected and used against him. In this sense soft does not mean weak, but yielding.

Sohei: Buddhist priests who were also trained in the martial arts during Japan's feudal period. They served to defend the monasteries in times of trouble, but often became involved in political disputes and more temporal matters.

Suieijutsu: Art of swimming, but included such skills as removing armour under water, swimming in full armour, and loosing arrows while in the water.

Sumo: Style of wrestling that is unique to Japan. It is a mixture of skill, religion and ritual dating back about 1,500 years. The wrestlers are of extremely large stature.

Sunakakebo: Oar or paddle used in the traditional martial arts of the Ryuku Islands.

Tachi: Japanese sword which has been mounted so that it can be worn suspended from the waist with the cutting edge facing uppermost. It was fashionable with the early mounted samurai and later became a popular way of carrying a sword for formal occasions.

Tae kwon do: Form of Korean karate, but differs from the Japanese style because more emphasis is placed on kicking techniques.

Tai-chi: Chinese martial art based on the soft internal styles of Taoism (q.v.). It was said to be founded by Chang San-feng as a defensive boxing system. Today, however, it is often taught for its therapeutic benefits.

Tanso: Short spear used in some traditional Japanese fighting styles. It was not a common weapon of the samurai but can be found in some schools of jujutsu such as Yagyu Shingan Ryu.

Tao: Traditional Chinese curved broadsword. The weapon is about 3 ft (1 m) in length and dates back to the Han dynasty.

Taoism: Religious philosophy attributed to the 2nd-century philosopher Chang Tao Ling. It reflects man's desire to find within himself the universal oneness of nature. The more nebulous character Lao Tzu established Taoism in the works called I-Ching.

Tare: Protector that goes around the waist in kendo. It is divided into three padded cloth plates with a backup of three other plates behind that. The tare is not a scoring area but protects the groin and lower areas.

Tatami: Mats made of rice straw about 3 ft × 6 ft (1 m × 2 m). Japanese use tatami in most traditional houses and rooms are measured by the number of tatami in them. In some martial arts such as judo, special tatami are put down to soften the hard falls.

Tate hiza: Seated posture used in some styles of iaido (q.v.). In Japan's feudal era and particularly towards the 18th century it became a popular way of sitting for the samurai class. In tate hiza the right leg rests under the buttocks and the left foot is brought next to it.

Tegasajutsu: Term used in the later styles of jujutsu (q.v.) and refers to the art of defence using the traditional Japanese umbrella.

Tekage: Steel claws that fit over each hand and are secured around the wrist. They were used by the ninja for climbing and clinging. Sometimes they would be used for defence if the ninja was suddenly attacked.

Tekko: Crude form of knuckle-duster employed during the feudal period in the Ryukyu Islands. The techniques used with the weapon were from Okinawa te and similar indigenous styles.

Tengu: Legendary Japanese mountain demons who lived in the ethereal world and had long noses and wings. The tengu were renowned as masters of the martial arts and in particular the sword.

Tessen jutsu: Art of using a fan for defence; usually the fan has iron ribs or is made of iron. Some classical Japanese styles of martial arts include this art in their repertoire. It is not a major skill of the samurai class.

Tetsubishi: Wide selection of spiked instruments used by Japan's feudal ninja. They were thrown down in clusters to slow down or stop pursuers. No matter how they fell, at least one spike would always remain pointing upwards.

Tetsubo: Battlefield staff covered with strips of iron and iron studs. Some types were made completely of iron. The tetsubo was used only by the very strong samurai who could wield it.

Titjio: Chinese weapon from the Hokkien people of Fukien consisting of a rod with a tine on either side. It may have been taken from China to the Ryukyu Islands, where the people developed their own techniques and called it sai (q.v.).

Tjabang: Metal-shafted weapon with tines either side of the handle. It comes from Indonesia and resembles the sai (q.v.) of the Ryukyu Islands. The tjabang is perhaps the earliest forerunner of this type of weapon.

Tobi kunai: Ninja housebreaking instrument used for opening bolted gates. It consists of a long pole with a forked blade.

Tonfa: Weapon from the Ryukyu Islands, originated from a rice grinding handle. It consists of a shaft, with a protruding grip at one end. It was used in pairs.

Tori: In prearranged forms of modern martial arts training, such as kata, the Japanese word tori refers to the person who completes the technique. Uke (q.v.) is usually the attacker and is defeated.

Torinawajutsu: Art of securing a prisoner with rope and also called hojojutsu. Was inherent to many classical styles of Japanese martial skills throughout the feudal era.

Trigrams: Early Chinese symbols consisting of three lines, some of which are broken and others whole. Each set of three lines represents an aspect of natural balance. For example, three solid lines represents the positive principle and three broken lines the negative principle.

Tsubogiri: Fork-shaped instrument used by the ninja of feudal Japan to bore spyholes in walls.

Tsuki: Term used in kendo for the throat, which is the target area protected by a strong leather pad which comes down from the men (helmet).

Tsurugi: Japanese term for a straight-bladed sword not made in the traditional way. Sometimes the term ken is also used to describe such a blade.

Ukata: Lightweight kimono often made of cotton, which is worn as casual wear during the hot and humid summers in Japan.

Uke: In Japanese martial skills, and in particular modern styles, uke is usually the person who initiates an attack in the prearranged kata (q.v.) forms of training. Because uke starts the attack, he is invariably the loser.

Ukidaru: Portable means of crossing a moat or river used by the ninja. It consisted of two wooden buckets, joined by cord. The ninja used a paddle called a shinobigai and with a foot in each bucket, paddled across the water.

Wakamusha and Wakato: Junior retainers to the samurai who carried swords and could defend their master.

Wakato: See Wakamusha

Wakizashi: Middle-length Japanese sword that was sometimes worn with the katana (q.v.) as a second weapon. It was only permitted to be worn in this way by high-ranking samurai during Japan's feudal period.

Wara zori: Japanese straw sandals that are used for outdoor wear. A thong slips between the big toe and the others and is tied with straw tapes around the ankles.

Watabi: Socks worn by the Japanese, which have only one split at the toes so that the big toe can slip through the thong of the wara zori (straw slipper). It was said that the first foreigners in Japan thought the Japanese only had two toes when they saw them wearing watabi.

Wing-chun: Chinese martial art from the south. Its foundation is attributed to Ng Mui, a nun from the Shaolin temple. The present grand master, Yip Man, had Bruce Lee as his student. The punching is very straight line and techniques called 'sticking hand' are part of its repertoire.

Wu-shu: Mandarin term which means the collective study of Chinese martial arts.

Yabusame: Japanese skill of archery on horseback. It can still be seen practised today when the exponents ride at great speed past a target and loose arrows into it.

Yadome: Art of blocking arrows fired at the exponent, and used by the samurai on the battlefield when they became the particular target of an individual archer. In modern times the skill of yadome is all but extinct, the Maniwa Nen Ryu being one of the few styles still to train in this discipline.

Yamabushi: Itinerant monks of Japan's feudal era who roamed the remote and mountainous areas. They were warrior priests (monks) and skilful in the martial arts. The ninja sometimes used the disguise of a yamabushi on his assignments.

Yari: Japanese spear that was a much-used weapon of the early samurai on the battlefield. Later the shaft became shorter and it was sometimes employed for defence of the samurai household. In modern times this weapon is seldom seen in martial arts.

Yawara: Japanese term used to describe a style of feudal empty-hand fighting, similar to jujutsu (q.v.).

Yin yang: The principle of opposites is represented by both the negative and positive. In China, the negative is called yin and the positive is called yang. In Japan these aspects of cosmology are called in and yo.

Yokozuna: Title given to the grand champions of sumo (q.v.).

Yoriki: Senior police officers in Japan's feudal police force, selected from samurai families.

Yoroi doshi: Armour-piercing dagger used by the samurai to despatch an armour-clad warrior in close-quarter combat.

Zazen: Seated meditative posture in either full or half lotus position, with the feet folded over the inner thighs.

Zen: Japanese name for religious philosophy attributed to the monk Bodhidarma and founded in the 6th century AD. In China it is called Ch'an. Its followers find enlightenment through direct experience and meditation, rather than by continual reading of the scriptures.

Zoshiki: Equivalent to the page of Western chivalry. They served the samurai but were not allowed to carry a sword (see also Chugen).

INDEX

Picture credits

Terry Allen, title page, back cover, 26-27, 30, 74-75, 95, 194, 196, 200; **Allsport,** 203; **P. Y. Bénoliel,** 165; **British Museum,** 8, 18-19, 60 top left and bottom, 65 top, 107 bottom, 116, 118-119, 120, 144, 154-155; **BBC Hulton Picture Library,** 58, 88, 89, 93 top, 98, 127; **Creative Cartography,** 15, 40-41 map (copyright Creative Cartography Ltd), 70 map (copyright Creative Cartography Ltd), 93 bottom, 129 top, 148; **Colorific!,** 137, 168-169; **Coloursport,** 7, 134, 157, 173; **Sylvio Dokov,** 166; **Mary Evans Picture Library,** 20 top, 38, 79, 97; **Michael Finn,** 24, 29, 80, 92, 93 bottom, 106, 107 top, 108-109, 110 both, 111 both, 113, 132, 140, 148, 149, 170, 177 top, 178, 182-183, 189, 192, 193 top, 201; **M. Jay,** 20 bottom, 104; **Arthur Tansley,** 22, 52, 55, 115 both, 121 top left and bottom, 128 bottom right, 129 bottom, 131, 142, 146, 152 bottom left, 153 bottom right, 158, 159, 160 both, 163, 164 both, 167 both, 172, 181 top, 185 both, 193 bottom; **Ulrich Hausman,** 10 both, 12, 13 both, 14, 39, 46 top, 48, 49, 60 bottom, 61 both; **Robert Harding Picture Library,** 186; **Michael Holford,** 16, 78, 138-139; **Hutchinson Library,** front cover, 57, 114, 121 top right, 136, 141 both, 171, 175, 177 bottom, 188, 202; **Kobal Collection,** 54; **Peter Lewis,** 161, 162; **Lee Yuen Subscription Agencies,** 43 bottom, 44, 56, 63 bottom, 65 bottom; **Mackenzie Publishing Ltd,** 15 right (artwork by Nick Skelton), 21, 112, 129 (artwork by Nick Skelton), 156, 174, 181 bottom, 184; **Manchester Museum,** 31; **Mansell Collection,** 11, 45, 46 bottom, 47; **National Geographic Magazine,** 99 (by James Stanfield); **M. Random,** 117, 126, 152 left; **Rex Features,** 36; **Spectrum Colour Library,** 190-191, 195; **Sporting Pictures,** 4, 176; **Supersport,** 153 bottom left, 204; **Eastern Images Picture Library,** 33, 66, 68, 69, 71, 73 right, 76, 77, 82, 83, 84, 86, 90; **Courtesy of the Trustees of the Victoria and Albert Museum,** 1, 35, 72, 73 left, 81, 88, 96, 100, 101; **Xinhua News Agency,** 43 top, 50, 53, 58, 60 top, 62, 63 top; **Japanese Foundation,** 91; **National Film Archive,** 94, 145.

Mackenzie Publishing Ltd and Stanley Paul & Co Ltd have made every effort to acknowledge every agency or photographer whose work has been used in this book.